SELECTED POEMS

James Applewhite

SELECTED POEMS

Duke University Press   Durham & London   2005

Printed in the United States of
America on acid-free paper ∞
Designed by CH Westmoreland
Typeset in Bembo by Tseng
Information Systems, Inc.
Library of Congress Cataloging-
in-Publication Data appear on
the last printed page of this book.

Duke University Press gratefully
acknowledges the support of the
Mary Duke Biddle Foundation,
which provided funds toward the
production of this book.

Contents

On the Selection

Selected Poems is divided into nine sections, which reflect the chronology of the nine published books. I have rearranged some of the material to represent the original contour of the earlier work. In the 1970s, my writing was often prompted by an occasion, a chance encounter while on foot or driving—or by a significant event, such as the death of a beloved figure, as in "William Blackburn, Riding Westward." Sometimes the encounter was simply with a thought in relation to a landscape, as in "Bordering Manuscript," written (pretty much as it is printed here) while in my car near the Law School of Duke University, after a walk across campus. I was also at work on a long poem using certain obsessively recurring memories of growing up in a small town in eastern North Carolina, in relation to tensions induced by the Vietnam war. This poem, "The War with My Father," engaged spiritual fatherhood, male identity models, and images of warfare, but never fully developed a language for mediating between the past and that present.

My feelings respecting male leadership in our culture, the divisions between spirituality and violence, projected themselves backward, into recollections of World War II versus the Christian quietism I had known, growing up in a Methodist household, son of a minister's daughter, with a pious grandfather and one maternal uncle a minister. I considered including the whole of "The War with My Father" as an appendix. But I wanted this volume to be based on published poems. Many memory-passages from the long poem *had* been published, as the last section of *Statues of the Grass* (University of Georgia Press, 1975). Some also appeared in later books. The occasion-prompted poems of the early 1970s made up most of *Statues of the Grass*, and are now represented in section I of *Selected Poems*. Section II puts back together, in their original sequence, all of the passages taken from "The War with My Father," which were published as individual poems.

Section III is selected from *Following Gravity* (University Press of Virginia, 1980). Donald Justice, judge of the 1979 Associated Writing Programs contest I had won, persuaded me to delete a group of poems I had written in England, while on a Guggenheim Fellowship. The manuscript of those poems remained in my imagination, and I present it here, as section IV. It is completed by a few poems written later and published in *Foreseeing the Journey* (LSU Press, 1983).

It would have been simpler to have selected each section from a single published book. But I have taken this opportunity to clarify issues—for myself, and hopefully for my readers—that were implicit in my first publications. In the first book, there was a certain vision, and a simple, direct way of putting it into words, which were the only language for the thing I then had to say. The poems were about identity in relation to place and involved a sense of familiarity and distance. They concerned an initiation into a culture, and a spiritual intuition of a selfhood, that seemed to stand *prior* to this eastern Carolina village and its passionate, collective-minded people, with their history-encoded attitudes toward ownership and race. The sequence I have reassembled as section II struggles especially with the strangeness of this encounter. This first self feels almost as if fallen from the sky, into this humid landscape and lineage. The meaning of his inheritance is partly that it is gratuitous, inexplicable. These folk may be rough-handed, harsh, inarticulately loving, but they are *his*. This is to be his home and his family. These seasons of tobacco farming, war work, gardening, the lengths of these Methodist sermons, are to create his sense of time. He seems to remember a larger, clearer, timeless perspective, just at the moment when he feels himself fully enveloped in this other, blood-related knowledge. Rereading "The War with My Father," I see that I then lacked a language for my contemporary anger over Vietnam, as it echoed against an earlier wonderment, and a sense of reluctance and acceptance. I could encode the conflicts I felt only in depicting the remembered moments. Still, the sequence of those self-encircled times moves into the present, as in "Keeper of the Dragon's Teeth."

Looking back over the nine books, I felt that they embodied an aspiration toward a more inclusive language. How could the lyrical, accepting voice of the first self expand and adapt, in response to the many alien experiences that time includes? As a poet, I have needed to be both innocent and experienced, and to find modulations of style connecting these conditions. If my linguistic journey is *about* time, as well as *into* time, perhaps I have been able to graph that ineffable subject experientially, without directly intending, through poems recording the landscapes of these many years. This thought guided my selection. Perhaps these poems, if rightly arranged, I hoped, might trace a trajectory of form and voice that developed along with the more complicated knowledges of career, marriage, fatherhood, friendships and enmities, of failing and succeeding, in the passage through what Blake called Experience.

Section V is taken from *Ode to the Chinaberry Tree and Other Poems* (LSU Press, 1986)—a book that adapts traditional English forms, such as ode and pastoral elegy, to the experience and language of eastern North Carolina. Section VI contains most of *River Writing: An Eno Journal* (Princeton University Press, 1988). This book, written during my last year as director of the Institute of the Arts at Duke University, began as a journal recording daily runs next to the Eno River, starting from behind my house, and eventually included a hiking excursion to the Grand Tetons. Appearing in the Princeton Series of Contemporary Poets (chosen by John Hollander), *River Writing* escaped the notice of my southern readers. I present it here essentially complete, continuing the dialectic between short poems and sequences, and between the near and the far, the present and the past. Written from the start as a single poem, it required no lifting out of shorter units from a longer context. The only selection to be made was from among the different days of the year recorded: mostly by drafts I would write in my head, while next to the river, running.

Section VII comes from *Lessons in Soaring* (LSU Press, 1989) and continues the exploration of landscapes in the present, with poems based on my experience as a student sailplane pilot, as well as on the time in Manhattan, with a semester-long arts program. Section VIII comes from *A History of the River* (LSU Press, 1993)—a book responding to the deaths of my wife's father and of my mother, and to the incapacity of my father, which obliged me to manage the family tobacco farm in Wilson County in his name, for six years. This meant an emotional homecoming, through an economic and cultural perspective, to the region that had first shaped me. Section IX comes from *Daytime and Starlight* (LSU Press, 1997), with the two final poems representing *Quartet for Three Voices* (LSU Press, 2002).

The obsessive issues are in some sense looked back on from afar: from a reminiscent, ruined farmhouse in northern Durham County; from a botanical recreation of a coastal pocosin in Chapel Hill, N.C.; from the perspective of astronomy; from a bridge across the Mississippi, in Minnesota; from a residence in the American Academy in Rome; from a sailboat off the North Carolina coast; from St. Peter's Square, glimpsing the pope; from an interstate highway near Washington, D.C.; from William Wordsworth's favorite perspective, above Lake Grasmere. The near landscape and the far seem part of a single topography: the slice of space-time I have known, viscerally, intellectually, running or hiking or canoeing or driving or sailing or sailplaning, over the years. The places in time marked out by the sections of this book appear closer together than I ever imagined they would, setting out. It is a partly continuous terrain, though with underground dynamics still to explore. Perhaps this book can be read as a single narrative, a story I have written with my life, across these years.

I continue the journey, and will continue these verbal records: these reports by the way, these poems that are shaped by the way, and that shape the way. Though I may think somewhat differently now, and look not nearly the same in photos, I still share a continuity of feeling with that original self. Sometimes, still, I experience his first-encountered community across the years as a kind of auditory vision. It may arise on seeing the houses of a small town or country crossroads, gathered near a cemetery hill slope, beside a lake or a river. Words then come into my inward hearing with the earlier emphasis, aligning me and that first self with our people, white and black, from places in the Midwest, or the Carolinas, or small-town New England. I feel us now riding the same planet, in human and astral time, around our local star. That first self and I will trace these arcs and orbits for a while longer, with wonder and thankfulness, part of a larger family, at home on a wider earth.

I

State Road 134

Down N.C. 134 past the township of Troy:
places not much in anyone's thoughts,
Wadesboro, Mt. Gilead, Calvary Church.
One yard spired
with the heartening thumb-bells of foxglove.
Road going past where the quick dog evaded
a truck in the monstrous heat: where
a hawk lay dead in a rumple of feathers,
a cow stood still under sweet gum scrub
and switched its tail.

I witnessed the chimney of a house long burnt
beside a ditchbank flooded with Cherokee rose.

And a field at my random turning
laid open and alone,
sky's rim back like an eyelid fringed
with the clay soil's fledgling pines.
Two board shacks with
windowpanes crushed by the heat,
paint bruised off by a weight of deprivation.

What balm of Gilead
descends for this mother, baby
on the hip of her luminous jeans?
In what hollow of mind
has even Christ held such features?

Face of a black boy vacant almost
as the country turning,
fields' loneliness sitting on his eyelids
too pure almost to be endured
in this forgetful distance.

My Grandfather's Funeral

I knew the dignity of the words:
"As for man, his days are as grass,
As a flower of the field so he flourisheth;
For the wind passeth, and he is gone" —
But I was not prepared for the beauty
Of the old people coming from the church,
Nor for the suddenness with which our slow
Procession came again in sight of the awakening
Land, as passing white houses, Negroes
In clothes the colors of the earth they plowed,
We turned, to see bushes and rusting roofs
Flicker past one way, the stretch of fields
Plowed gray or green with rye flow constant
On the other, away to unchanging pines
Hovering over parallel boles like
Dreams of clouds.

                      At the cemetery the people
Surprised me again, walking across
The wave of winter-bleached grass and stones
Toward his grave; grotesques, yet perfect
In their pattern: Wainwright's round head,
His bad shoulder hunched and turning
That hand inward, Luby Paschal's scrubbed
Square face, lips ready to whistle to
A puppy, his wife's delicate ankles
Angling a foot out, Norwood Whitley
Unconsciously rubbing his blue jaw,
Locking his knees as if wearing boots;
The women's dark blue and brocaded black,
Brown stockings on decent legs supporting
Their infirm frames carefully over
The wintry grass that called them down,
Nell Overman moving against the horizon
With round hat and drawn-back shoulders —
Daring to come and show themselves
Above the land, to face the dying

Of William Henry Applewhite,
Whose name was on the central store
He owned no more, who was venerated,
Generous, a tyrant to his family
With his ally, the God of Moses and lightning
(With threat of thunderclouds rising in summer
White and ominous over level fields);
Who kept bright jars of mineral water
On his screened, appled backporch, who prayed
With white hair wispy in the moving air,
Who kept the old way in changing times,
Who killed himself plowing in his garden.
I seemed to see him there, above
The bleached grass in the new spring light,
Bowed to his handplow, bent-kneed, impassive,
Toiling in the sacrament of seasons.

Driving through a Country America

It begins to snow in a country
Between the past and what I see,
Soft flakes like eyelids softly descending,
Closing about branches, orchards of pecans,
Like washpot soot streaked in lines on the sky

Or is it that these husks empty of nuts
Are moving upward among the flakes they have suspended,
Like eyesockets gaping or a mockery of birds

So that a girl by the name of Mary Alice Taylor
Sings across this air from the seventh grade.
"Billie he come to see me. Billie he come
Last night." A mole, color of clear skin,
Swims by her nose. Flakes condense the light.

"Billie he asked me to be his wife, 'course I said alright."

Snow as if holding the country houses
Apart to be inspected, unsilvered
Mirror that lets float out of its depths
As from an old ocean of no dimension
Unlimited objects, leather tack and
Spokes of surreys, china
Long broken, whittled horses
Everything their hands would have touched.

The Sunplane

Upper Room rusts religiously into the Reader's Digest.
Jesus is praying, a light is about his countenance.
Catalogues of hardware promote lawnmowers and speedboats.
Sunlight circles with specks: yellow for these pages.
One whole cluttered story is devoted to the wreckage
Of childhood. Chemistry sets, ball bats, wasps' nests.
The thread of my labyrinth begins somewhere in there,
In the control-line model I never made fly or in the Cleveland
Kit of a Stinson Reliant which is still unbuilt.
Its plans are clear and full-sized, the scale exact,
The balsa twigs still yellow, crumbly, and light.
I could build its skeleton still as from a fist full of beams,
To rise on the tissue I now know how to shrink taut
Toward an early-morning sun. I'd have no hesitation
In leaving the house, dew I'd mark with my feet
Shows no single step back. The motor is turned
By solar batteries of silicon, the most powerful for their weight,
That I've ordered from Edmund Scientific. Steadily as sunlight
Rises, the Stinson rises, clearing the slender
Little trees edging in the ball diamond's outfield
(A small enough space to fly models in), leaving below
In the past one moody boy with a hand-launch glider,
As the Stinson rises reliant on wings of all things
I've labored to learn since then, and lay now in offering
Before those unsatisfied hours, my forehead brooding
In a bramble outfield, whose trees' names I couldn't untangle.

O Stinson I build you yet! Rise with the light.

Leaf Mirrors

Along a dustless clay road in wet weather,
　　　from the wide leaves there radiates
a presence of coolness and green, like water.

And the field of white weeds, delicate
　　　flattened umbrellas or mushroom heads;
Queen Anne's lace, so nearly flowers,

white sprays of unkempt blossom
　　　cocked in numberless angles to one another,
strung as if by invisible attraction

to the scattered clouds; and those soft-brushed
　　　billows seem deeply filamented,
potential with rain. Such

water-mirroring leaves ineffably unite
　　　with clouds in this light deepened by haze,
like trees regarding their figures in a pond.

The cloud-strung weeds, leaved clouds, shimmering
　　　holding a water-depth, connection
like consciousness, diminish

me shaped into the mosaic foliage,
　　　summer that is summer by passing; but mirror
my shared life between them, beyond me; suggest.

William Blackburn, Riding Westward

Here in this mild, Septembral December, you have died.
Leaves from the black oaks litter our campus walks,
Where students move, or stand and talk, not knowing
Your wisdom's stature, illiterate in the book of your face.

So often we walked along the old stone wall at night,
Looked up at your window, where lamplight cleft your brow,
And knew you were suffering for us the thornier passages,
Transfixed by *Lear*, or staring ahead to the heart
Of Conrad's Africa. Sometimes we ventured inside,
To be welcomed by an excellent whiskey, Mozart's *Requiem*.
This clarity of music and ice revealed once in air
A poem as you read it: as Vaughan created "The World,"
Eternity's ring shining "calm as it was bright."

On a wall was the picture of you riding on a donkey,
Caught in mid-pilgrimage, to a holy land I do not remember.
But your missionary parents had birthed you in Persia,
And after we'd learned that, we saw you as explorer;
From hometowns scattered on an American map marked
Terra incognita for the heart, you led treks
Into our inward countries, and still seem discovering before,
Through straits to "the Pacific Sea," or the "Eastern riches."
Left on these New World shores – so thoroughly possessed,
So waiting to be known – on all sides round we see
Great trees felled and lying, their bodies disjoined,
Or standing in all weather, broken, invaded by decay.

The worn landscape of your features, the shadows
Days had cast under eyes, were part of the night
That steadily encroaches on the eastward globe, as it rotates
In sunlight. Out of your age shone a gleam of youth,
Which seems with cedars' searing to sing in the forest
In wolf's ears of green flame.

                              Still, you are dead.
Your system is subject to entropy. Cells' change

Reduced your monarchial features to a kingship of chaos.
"With faltering speech, and visage incomposed,"
You said good night, between pangs of the withering hunger
Which filled your dying dreams with apples and cheeses.

In spite of the revolt of your closest ally, your body,
You died with the nobility you'd taught, and teaching, learned.
And now you roam my brain, King Lear after death.
The broken girl in your arms is only your spirit,
A poor fool hanged by Cordelia, by the straits of fever.
We visit your old office on campus in grief.
Outside, trees lift winterward branches toward
A sky in chaos. The patterning which spins the stars
Exists outside this weather we live under.

We see only branches against those clouds' inclemency.

Looking for a Home in the South

I

This particular spring day, March 19, 1973,
Is tearing at itself with insanities of traffic. Trucks
Of construction components, trucks of concrete, bulk like what is real.
I try to look through this particular day as through the doorframe of an
    abandoned house.
Squinting around the foreground, the shoulders of metal, I glimpse
Where apple tree boughs in wind strummed washboard clapboard.

II

Closer home, the tin on barns rusts as with a memory of mules.
A few houses cling, through camellias and columns, to an illusion,
Whose substance of grace never ruled within a South which existed.
But where is this land, which showed to our old ones as an horizon
    in the future,
And now, for us, is secret in the hovering of the past?

Was it a sap which awoke from grassroots snapped at plowing?
Even now the broken-top trees tap down into a soil below this moment.
The juice of it tightens around bulbs, squeezing up jonquils, wild onions.

III

Off the highway and almost there, tobacco barns and houses are bare to
    the sky.
A sparrow hawk has leaped from the light wire, leaving me balancing
In a wind that is chilled between hurt and delight.
My great grandfather's stone looks white from his iron-fenced graveyard
The color of briars, the fields that he keeps in his watch are combed with
    new furrows.

IV

This particular spring day, over which we are constructing despair
With materials of depression and concrete, the land we have missed lies
    hidden—
Trickles and glistens in the dark, radiant to roots. Will none of us
Live to live into the unalloyed sunshine this land would learn to give us?

Discardings

Sometimes going back toward together I find
Me with lost, no-count, low-down and lonely:
Single with trees in logged-over evening,
Sun on us bound to go down.

Things lying low are sipped by the weather.
Black-strap creeks seem a slow molasses
Toward horizons thirsty with gravity.

Today in trees I kicked an old bucket
Full of woes, the chipped enamel like knotholes.
Burrows raised lids under leaves; quick fur
Eyes were on my face. Under the trash pile
I heard them like trickles of water,
Tunneling the sun down.

Home, when I pour bourbon and remember
A holed rubber boot on a hill of leaves,
It must be their sounds I am drinking.

I salute a boot from the foot
Of an unheralded cavalry. A black man
Walked furrows behind a mule whole years, unhorsed
By no war but the sun against the moon.

I drink branch water and bourbon
To the boards of his house that the wind
Has turned to its color and taken entirely.

Visit with Artina

She lives in a house whose color is bone left out
In the weather, over-lap siding gone pallid as wood ash.
A sheen condenses out of air on the polished grain.
Three little ones, their hair braided up in corn-rows,
Flock at her skirts, touch hands to her knees for comfort.
She is seventy, rake-handle thin, her shanks are bowed,
Her hip is troublesome ("some days I jes can't go");
Peculiar highlights luminesce on her cocoa skin.
Her hands are white inside, and shape whatever
She says in the air, or touch her three to be good.

"That ten dollars a week I used to get—I was study'en on it
Yesterday. I raised Joseph, Bernice, Wilma Doris, and theirs,
An they didn't never go hungry, we always had more
Than cornbread and greens 'a sett'en on the stove" (lives
Of collard greens pile high in the room) "I did it, Lord,
And now I feel good, jes like the little birds 'a sailing
In the air" (her fingers are bones for believable wings).

"Back when I worked for your folks—I felt burdened down,
Like everybody else was higher." The right hand hovers
Over the left, in a different world. "For three years I dreamed
This dream, when I got down sick. It was all a dark cloud."
One palm wipes the air full of darkness over
The plastic flowers, the brown-earth sofa. "And a great crowd
Of people. They was troubled, trouble was among 'em.
I was to lead 'em, I was among 'em but I was apart.
I walked in the middle between 'em but I was far off."
Her hands have quarried cloud-pillars from the troubled air.
"An so I could get 'em there, he gave me a star."
One sure finger, in all the blue spaces of her room,
Picks out this point, maybe floating lint or a sungrain
Alone, places it, a star, in the middle of her forehead.
"An my mother, an my grandmother, what was Mothers in the church;
I 'scerned 'em on a hill, a way off." Her palms smooth the air.
She makes white robes with her palms. "I 'scerned 'em on a hill."

"These were the words that were give me: 'by the grace of God
I shall meet you.'" The house of her skin is strangely sheened,
Like sky-reflection polishing boards, or color
Rain water has caught from the air, in whatever low place.

A Kid at the County Fair

Cocoons tasted sweet on cones, potatoes fried,
Squeals squeezed out of girls as a Bomber dived.
Rita Moreno's lids made slits. Her offer
Boiled down to this: we'd eye her tits for a quarter.
A sign on a silver trailer where the spotlight's tongue
Touched the night told of a girl in an iron lung.
We gave to go in. She lay in a metal cylinder
Moved at the foot convulsively by a metal lever.
Face under shadow, she surrendered herself to its breath
That hissed. Outside, I sensed the arc-light spit
And erect its column, each particle electric, separate.
The motorcycle mounting centrifugally in the "Drum of Death"
Turned the fair in a vortex. I stepped to earth, intent
On a wound. Air moved coarse between my teeth,
Atoms of electricity and grease. I walked from the accident.

Revisitings

The sky is low and close and light is a mist.
Sunday makes shine a still more sultry water
In this summer air. Grass returns prodigal with seed.
These birds that perk and skip seem living souls.
Magnolia flowers are reminiscent of childhood and candles.
Past a line inscribed on leaves by a bobwhite's whistle,
I suspect a different self like a nobler brother.
Mimosa trees in flower, piles of clouds
In an horizon without perspective, help me recall.
I sit on the hill of an avenue of trees, feeling
That I want to say hush, hush, to the traffic.
For a little while I feel close again to a person
Who one time existed under immensely tall trees.
A wind from where shadows are generating rain tells me
This day stands always in pools behind doors I have closed.
How have I closed away my best self and all of his memories?
Many of the tongues of grass are speaking to the sun,
Obscured for a moment, in a language of vapor from underneath.

Zeppelin Fantasy

I fly on the Hindenburg, though last night
My dreams were of flame. Inside the sound
Of motors is an aluminum piano. Its icy
Tones bare teeth of diamond, whose grin
Chills the bosom of an American heiress.
Languages are eaten with a salad of medals
By the satin stripes of trousers. Girders
As elliptical as sleep invent our night
Above the Atlantic. We dance in a dream
Like a politician's black cigar.

Bordering Manuscript

I am alert to these letters in extraordinary numbers: perhaps
      from grass heavy-headed with seed, flickering a's and r's
under pressure of sun that I recognize as holy and intended—
      while a bird of indecipherable mind is scrolling margins of air.
A gold, illegible word rests on the left hand of vision.
      Illusions of its spelling leaf from the lacquer of hedges past
exits of buildings. Women removed across hundred-foot stretches
      of chained grass evoke vowels with their liftings of hair,
but let me confess: the name could be a man's as well as a woman's.
      People printed with my children and wife in the foreground, though
accurate and clear, seem from a sufficient, forgetful distance
      to twine into the gigantic characters which fit no speech.
Places redolent with heat and resinous pines of meetings
      perhaps ten years ago form amber in retrospect;
the puzzle I see has thousands of pieces, each poor day
      hiding its two or one. Had I all the days permanently together,
I could assemble the jig-sawed chips in a lifetime. This thought
      chills me close to a water-like stillness, tea-colored and brackish
with vacations on rivers, as if a plane of focus shimmering behind
      the tear in a photograph, or body of air from all fields
inhabiting a music. Behind my lips, tipping my unknown
      tongue, she waits in her surface, her name my speech's mistress.

To Alexander Solzhenitsyn, in Exile

Safe in the West, you will be watched over henceforth
By citizen press and police, officials elected
Through only our typical corruptions, administrators of hospitals
Where in your declining years these deeds will buy you
Easy entrance if then you are rich and remembered.

Our wire services distort your words, your bearded face,
Bleared from primitive terror in Russia the mother,
Is ironically represented by these crowding photographs.
Some will suspect, once you are tarnished by quick
Years of news, your noble treason not notable after all,
Since they have allowed you to live, it appears. But exile,
In your case, fits a capital offense. I imagine
Faulkner banished from the South he passionately confessed,
Whitman forbidden to walk the streets of his comrades' Manhattan.
No, your crime was grave, and you have been desperately punished.
Your treachery was true, and now you must wander your days
Past averted eyes in mirrors of newsprint, glimpsing
Burlesques of your face caged with the vended pages.

Henceforth you walk as a writer on the soil that is sealed
In your head, now you must be both roots and their landscape,
Oh may you wander a vast and fertile Russia of memory.
Another martyr's victory of conscience is won,
For you have forced them, fighting you, to lie openly again:
They have told you that your land is not your land.

War Summer

In our tin-roofed house in the big war's summer,
In a somnolent town in sunlight's dominion,
I read of the Shalott of Lord Tennyson,
Dreaming beyond the guardrooms of the distant thunder
To a city in that sun's blind center.

How odd in my upstairs room, awake
In attic air, in wrath of the sun,
Except for my balsa Spitfire, alone,
Unable to descend, where my father'd mistake
My desire as he massed his jaws at steak.

Would that ardor of sunflame never relent?
My thoughts were a web as in the Lady's tower.
Tinkering tissue and sticks toward the power
Of flight, I dreamed all communion as ascent.
Our rapport in combat came only at twilight.

Through rumble of distant thunder, far
Flash of the six o'clock news. Under each
Portentous cloud, we turned from our workbench
Stunned. Radio's drone warned static; came roar
Above houses, artillery of a wide atmosphere.

A Southern Elegy

April, 1974

I

To picture the authentic locality of Lee's reputation:

Was it corn-stubble cabins, columns bemused by the ridges
In mindless Tennessee? Along the snake-winding mahoganies
Of the Chickasaw, the Pee Dee, the Chickahominy, the Haw,
    the Susquehanna?

Moss in beards, arthritic knees of cypresses, would have soughed
Of the fitness of his courses without a motion of breath.
Bass-fat lakes, scummed over with gore of sunsets,
Would ruminate victory in an atmosphere loaded with thunder.

Parisian silhouettes in the ballrooms of Richmond,
Locomotives' funnels on Petersburg sidings,
Were by themselves insufficient to hew out a polished space
From swampland oblivion, whose elegists were only mosquitoes.
The wonder is that names emerged at all
From such quicksand states and counties of woodland,
With such unthinkable horseback miles to cover:
Sloughs into which Hannibal and all his elephants might fall.

II

The voice of FDR, grave with Pearl Harbor,
Echoed along hallways of radio to threatened California.
What electricity of rumor overarched horizons
When Lee bestrode Traveller at Gettysburg?

Our minds are suspended from beacon to guyed beacon
In words across the sunsets, Sherman in diesel rigs
Rumbles this present day to our sea, Atlantas
Of pine trees fall to the chain saw's ricochet.

III

A stage expands above farms, electrons' phosphor
Over trees and streams, the gatherers of earliest mists,
Above crests still swollen with breastworks.
Towering names remain, casting like shadows
The absences of figures: misguided McClellan, A. P. Hill,
Sheridan and Stuart with cavalry toward Richmond.
Forrest, Longstreet, Pickett of Cemetery Ridge.

A stony Grant, rigidly on horseback, photographed, faces
The stovepipe height of Lincoln in rumple-leg dignity:
One figure equal in dimension to his legitimate theater.

The luminous eye of Lee is gone, with jaw-line of honor
And resolve. Fanatical intensity of Jackson is missing.

Lee. Lincoln. As Nixon jowls our land's automatic eye.

II

The Capsized Boat

I

My father was launching his speedboat
Through vines by the bridge.
Dark bottomed clouds were walking the sky.
Wet air enfolded like cloth, looked
Glassy in light between trees. Mosquitoes,
Drenched in the leaf-smell,
Tangled like creepers. Hard cold drops
From a shade that moved higher than trees' shade
Had spattered the stream.

II

After the shower I jumped for the cockpit.
The stern wave of another speedboat challenged our passing.
We crowded the creek with our thunder
All the way from Ruffin's Bridge. Father crouched before
The Evinrude motor. He drove by his desire
Our red prow across the slant wave.
I faced deep into a clammy sigh of water, which clung
Across the light and went cold.
Father pulled me alive from that odor of dying,
Swam up under the capsized boat
And saved me to my name. His overalls
Heavy with money, he hauled me into light of his example.

On the Homefront

I

Plate glass gazed on the depot. Auto parts wholesale.
Air brakes' coughs in switchyards, odor of metal.
A vacuum draws me: the wake of my father's words.

Nothing would be well said or ill, for order was by number:
So little part for me to play, I seem not present
In the memory.
                            Down the known aisles shelved to their ceilings,
We'd break upon a cave of mechanics, who bent in surrounding
Some motorblock open like a sacrificed carcass: hapless,
Greased. Plates and containers were set everywhere.
Unpalatable fluids. The point of the calendars were pictures,
Pinup poses, nipples like the fuses of shells
Or nacelles of aircraft. An *artist's conception*. She reflected
Blessings onto hoods from the enameled tones of her limbs.

II

Preparation of a meal of oil. Everyone
Wiping his hands with mill waste, secretly pleased.
She on the calendar curved sleeker than metal.
The sizes of bolts were language.
These pale inner-temple mechanics, during daylight,
Practiced the refinement of cylinder and piston.

A Vigil

I

Thanksgiving sacrament, piety of crystal and silver.
Platters and dishes passed on from hand to hand.
Words so well-worn they drone with the summertime fan.
My grandfather blessing, his countenance fields in the sunlight.

I waited beside him for words, for what he'd gathered
From hawks wheeling sun, oak leaves' tension under glare.
He rocked in the parlor with a bible, his face grown taciturn,
The hooked nose Indian, hair as if filamented down.
His parchment skin was the season's hieroglyphic.
Going for water, I passed through the company parlor:
Mantel with mirror and clock, stiff plush and varnish.

II

One window overlooked the creek, where silt
From high water on leaves seemed dust from days passing by.

I poured from a pitcher. Tracing a beaded trickle,
Sweat down a frosted tumbler. Sensation of October
In August. I thirsted to bring into potable solution
These motes of dust that swam the green shade's sunbeam.
I sat on the porch beside him, spell-bound by columns.
Horizon woven to softening by orbits of swallows.

"It's been eighty-six years and it seems like a day."

A Garden's Season

Divided from it now by this distance, I see our garden
Beyond or between these simple things which cannot define it.
Air outdoors and for children but crossed by gleams
From the Thanksgiving silver. Within a high board fence, where
    grandmother's
Roses were bordered with bricks. Where we played in the dirt.

The place of our dream remains tangent, though I recall
Also a concrete fish pond, a tree beside it
Either always in blossom or with cherries showing perfect as marbles.

Gold fish hung from the surface like impressions of flame.
Shadows passed over of a little girl and boy:
First selves I see as in an Easter-time photograph.

With fronded hair like the hyacinths, she dressed in velvet.
Like fish in those tones of silver and a rose, we swam
In the high wall's shadow, its atmosphere our drink and shelter,
Food to our mouths with Thanksgiving crystal and cherries.

II

Its trunk grown thick with our grandfather's years, the pecan
Waved above, like the upstairs rooms high as clouds;
Dried sage and furniture, frames to stretch curtains,
Would wait for us there until we'd ever have need of them,
Probably forever. Clouds moved over like wind across a pond,
Printing our faces with foliage they rippled.

Iron River

I was taken to a cousin's on the Pamlico River. Through old trees
I looked along moldering streets to the riverfront sunk
Below sunlight. Hulks wallowed mud among the weeds.
Sidewalks stank to my thoughts with imminent water.

I settled, exiled upstairs in a house held hostage
On its lower story by swirl and brown eddy; stuffed feathers
I picked from my pillow into an emptied cold cream jar,
To be tossed like a castaway's bottle from this tower window.
I bunched soap bubbles in a bowl like grapes, straw stem
Joining them still to my breath, so that rainbow membranes
Jointed like a lung would move with my chest.
                                              Later,
A vacation house of the Broughams', bare rooms, eyed pine.
Drumming of the tugs at night re-echoed like war.
Mazie and Aunt Elsie talked, while pines brushed the screens,
In an unfamiliar pungence of tone, of Haywood, Haywood Brougham.
This man's complexion sounded the color of broom sedge, his breathing
A rustle. Brougham, Brougham, with the night's cannonading
Of tugs, Haywood and his lungs, deadly *sanatorium*.

With Darkening Foliage

Recovering from rheumatic fever, I lay on our side porch couch,
An uncle to read to me. Tobruk, Rommel, Montgomery, El Alamein.
I was as pleased with the North Africa campaign as with our lawn
Attracting evenfall and dew with level-cut tuft,
Releasing soaked-in light in lightning bugs' effervescence.
I hung on his words by the bulb as they lanterned into our old pecan
Topheavy with darkening foliage. I remember a desert soldier
As equipped in *Mechanix Illustrated*: his pack his boots his Thompson gun,
These articles of invulnerable mastery. Remember now the photographs
Sensationalizing thought: the twin-boom P-38 test-firing
At night, tracers of its machine guns and cannon a fiery sword.
I suffered no doubt of these heroes' nature. They were Americans,
Righteous, and were brave. Night winds lashing the pecan
Past my window, explosions of summer storms' lightning,
Were atmospheres no more sweeping in tone than their anger and power.

Diamond of Shadow

It is the gray quiet fall of evening.
Dew is on the ball diamond stubble. We are
Bound for trees only more humped and shaped
To be hill-top still than the clouds,
Past the encircling outfield, over our knees in grass-shadow.
I have taken the next step and have fallen from my name,
Am behind or outside our occasion,
An odd thought only, absorbed in strangeness.

Expanding from that point and that moment,
I felt a radiant separation, sight without eyes
Over my own body's shoulder: me lost
In my footsteps, remembering as another.

A Forge of Words

I

Moths crowded streetlights revival evenings. The teenaged
Lingered long outside, reluctantly gathered.
The first hymn calling to sinners, bitter-mellow and lonesome,
Would detach us one by one from circumferences of light:
Circumscribed with shadow by a brim of tin, through leaves
Minnow-live in the wind. Still free among moths, we scraped
The wet sidewalk with reluctant soles, our shoulders flickered over
By magnified wings, like fluttering shapes of our sins.

At last to resist no longer we moved up concrete
Steps, abandoning the afternoon's rain in our thoughts,
To chastise our gesture, flip away bravado like cigarettes.

II

To gather up later. Now to fit sensibly in a pew.
I see my thighs muscled wide in the trousers.
The reverend's eyesockets hollow out under eventime lighting.
We weight his voice with our responses; as we bend in singing
We empower his beseeching.

                         Kneeling in shame at the altar,
I sense on the back of my neck that repentance is for women.
I turn and encounter the resolve in masculine faces.
Bill Tyson's leather folds and slab-flat cheeks
From his road-building weather. John Grimsley an ashed-over coal,
His face to front the seasons of farming unabashed
By salvation. My own father's jaws locked tight on the names
Of his sins, hardly bowed on his wrestler's neck;
This company of Christians grim like underworld gods.

From the anvil of Christ, I receive my hammered name.

Combat Station

Ralph with the corded triceps, with cleft chest wired
With black hair, told Marine Corps war. I wielded the spanner.
Our lift in the open sun made all metal stinging
In heat-thin oil. His talk was Australian women,
Severed American heads on a path in New Guinea.
The lens of an August atmosphere focused our labor.
Beads of tractors' rims were loosened with wedges.
We greased the trailers and pickups, washed clay rivers
From rusted fenders in the waning afternoons.
At his headquarters desk where a cash register rang,
My father gave orders to receive new assaults of customers.
We fought against being overrun, held wave after wave,
Fired slugs into chassis from the automatic greasegun,
My brother riddling fenders with a high-pressure hose.
No matter how we mauled at wedges, levered with tire tools,
Tugged at exhaust pipes blazing like machine guns,
Our general denied us victory by selling to the enemy.
Like heroes we fought for a stalemate, held out for sundown.
Staring into hubcaps, I remembered the metal of a P-47
That had cut through a grove of pines and broken in a field,
Pilots' blood jellied in the cockpit. My father's silhouette
Tightened the close-ringed horizon of trees, as I fought on
For the moment we could signal a roof above the gas pumps
To blaze up its pantheon of bulbs into creek-water evening,
When field moths would orbit their wattage like foliage in motion.

To Forgive this Inheritance

I

Sundays, I pushed through hedges, crossed ditches by fields.
In a water–shimmer atmosphere of heat, a clapboard church
Gleamed its steeple as white as Lot's salt wife.
I was not my father, not like him, I knew an intenser
Prayer than his. I had whispered it Saturday night
In my hard–won car on a dirt road that ran past trees.
Dark had been the cocoon for our tentative stirrings,
Air an elastic scented with corn.
Moths over fields bore us up on their cumulative wings.

II

Sun wedged pincers of light through the bases of clouds.
My grandfather had stood in his pew and prayed for rain,
Asking a blessing on farmers dressed by the weather.

I passed cornblades on ridges curling to tubes.
My vision through the clear air distilled its water,
A few drops thudded like bullets into the soil.
I felt the sky's blue curve alive as a skin,
Turned toward creek and the rich thrusts of trees.
Overcast, gathering in swirls, had moistened the sun.
A few drops circled the mahogany polish of the stream.

My eye, through answered prayer, grasped the lean fish
Under images of cloud upon water stable as stones.

Images, Burning

I

I stumbled from the university library, blind with images
Of the Messerschmitt. The frail dissertation refused to progress.
Fantasies of war, actual as iron, obstructed
My notebooks. The learned doctors inhabited crumbling
Centuries, towers which toppled into the Battle of Britain.
Sunlight lay with a tigerish gleam on the innocent grass.

II

Reading of war, I learn of the casualties:
Brave men trapped by canopies, in airplanes on fire.
The Spitfires, the Messerschmitts, spin toward the sunlit sea
Or island below like leaves from the tree of man.
Imagination expands in gratitude to fact
That each white down must parachute its seed,
The kernel living or not, back into a green map.

A Minister, Crippled

I

And S. E. clenched his jaws against mockery,
The pain that came soon, but without bitterness or vexation
In his lips' good lines, these lit always from within
By tunes of hymns he carried in his baritone humming.
I see him toiling from the back hall basin after shaving
To the chair in his study with extended legs,
A grown-up's highchair with legs of iron pipe,
Iron legs to ease his knobbed knees permanently crooked,
This spirit most upright among us bent to a cane.
I see him backing from a driveway, his neck as though
Stiffened by a military collar, watching through the mirror awkwardly,
Not able, like a child, to look over his shoulder.
And I as a child could with difficulty admire
His ministry and pain. I see him not in a pulpit
But in the domestic undress of his sickness, I hear
The resonance of his only male power, his voice,
Consoling the dreariness of a late-morning parsonage.
I recall him with the smells of soap and shaving, scents
Too like Easter lilies. I see the fine dark eyes
Uplifted toward a ceiling in an odor of plaster.

II

Upstairs in S. E.'s parsonage, a winter day.
Tall windows are fragile with the overcast light,
With sheen of a snow half-fallen and
Hidden by their ledges. Curled in the great white country
Of a mattress and sheets, I am at peace
In the world of Silvertip, wolf of the north.
I cannot explain how his savage nobility,
His ears like evergreens spiring from snow drifts,
Have flavored and altered the pallor of sickness.
I see S. E. become young and whole, my healed heart
Rides in his chest, beneath the blouse of a Canadian
Mounted Policeman so just as only a child could conceive.
All hills feel the perilous snow:
A pure cold, like the pearly teeth of a wolf.

Keeper of the Dragon's Teeth

Tuned by contemplation, I crest a hill road
In the Uwharrie forest, first see bloom the flame
Which had plumed before my climb in a dark-tree cloud.
I join a young ranger watching to hold the fire
Between a ravine to the right of us and this nook of our road.
As wind swells changing, he runs to unreel hose
Toward a new blaze to our left and I lope downslope toward
Dragonteeth men, marching as if springing out of earth,
Which the sparks have sewed. As I stamp upon
Half-black broom sedge and leaves lavender-rimmed with ignition,
The magical element tonguing my trousers my boots
Is orange on this overcast day.
It is only by my sidewise sweeping kicks of dirt
And rocks that these blazes are stayed. With an odor of burning
On boots and shirt, and the drying of fresh sweat upon me,
Water is sweet from a canteen. I stand by the ranger
While he speaks of the certainty of arson. Farmers drive past
In pickups, pig fat forearms hooked over windowledge.
I watch him calculating which one must have set it.
I am happy to stand for a time by a professional manager
Of the dragontooth element, stand for a few more words
Before walking up a ridge which overlooks the Uwharrie hills
Like a snake's folds rising out of water.
I sit upon a rock to the harping of the winds of thought
Till it is a very long way to the back of my neck
And I feel, beyond my shoulders, voices moving silently as daylight.

Boundary Stones

I scrub till the square of an old iron fence
Begins to come clear. Rust-eaten railing
Like a flaking cinder. I sweep out briars,
Am delicate about cutting the young trees.

Star-winking tangle of the slick briar leaves.
Sunlight timeless as creation. Birds
And dew and their voices sweeter than droplets
On each day dawning the beginning.

My great-great grandfather's shaft is tilting awry
And clasped by vines. I break the dry tendril.

Candle of stone. Its flame
On top the years of sun.

Henry Applewhite
Born October 3, 1801
Died November 29, 1849
Orphia wife of Henry Applewhite
Born October 21, 1806
Died August 11, 1896
Our mother and father are gone but not forgotten.

Stone condensed from a history of weather.

I place three heads of wheat from the field
Outside on the gravestone of each. Mourning doves
And bobwhites are calling; a sprinkling
Like early raindrops at the edges of cloud.

III

Tobacco Men

Late fall finishes the season for marketing:
Auctioneers babble to growers and buyers.
Pickups convoy on half-flat tires, tobacco
Piled in burlap sheets, like heaped-up bedding
When sharecropper families move on in November.

No one remembers the casualties
Of July's fighting against time in the sun.
Boys bent double for sand lugs, bowed
Like worshippers before the fertilized stalks.
The rubber-plant leaves glared savagely as idols.

It is I, who fled such fields, who must
Reckon up losses: Walter fallen out from the heat,
Bud Powell nimble along rows as a scatback
But too light by September, L.G. who hoisted up a tractor
To prove he was better, while mud hid his feet—
I've lost them in a shimmer that makes the rows move crooked.

Wainwright welded the wagons, weighed three
Hundred pounds, and is dead. Rabbit was mechanic
When not drunk, and Arthur best ever at curing.
Good old boys together—maybe all three still there,
Drinking in a barn, their moonshine clearer than air
Under fall sky impenetrable as a stone named for azure.

I search for your faces in relation
To a tobacco stalk I can see,
One fountain of up-rounding leaf.
It looms, expanding, like an oak.
Your faces form fruit where branches are forking.
Like the slow-motion explosion of a thunderhead,
It is sucking the horizon to a bruise.

A cloud's high forehead wears ice.

Drinking Music

I

Cornstalks and arrowheads, wood rot cleanly as wash
Hung in wind. They are covered by this roof as I think:
The losers, the fallen, the kind who go under, faces
As familiar as Civil War casualties to the soil's imagination.
Whiskey workers with no front teeth, men from down home,
With leather boots made by the *Georgia Giant*, denim or khaki
Their only other clothes, the dye scrubbed away
By brush in fields and seasons of laundry
So a sand white cotton shines through.

They stand for the showing of true colors, on soil
Instilled with the sun's going down, which crests up
At evening in a brick hue of broom sedge, clots below
In sweet potatoes succulent as blood.

Their ears give over to a jukebox excuse poured
Slow as molasses. Hank Williams' whiskey forgiveness.
The twang has a body like tenderloin and turnips.
Paul Junior Taylor, with your Budweiser belly,
Your shoulders muscled wide like a tackle's,
I wonder what it's done with you now.

II

The broom sedge fields were ruddy from sunset.
Cold whiskey is the color of straw.
Sky ain't hardly kept no color at all,
And Lord I'm lonely for the ground.
I'm far from home but near.
I'm high, so high and low. Sweet chariot.

The song is red, like what men eat.
Sky is clear as the ninety proof shine they drink.
Lord, Lord, a man is a funny piece of meat.
Their boots print fields that understand their feet.

Building in the Country

These fields toward the river are outside time.
The horse has been grazing forever.
That black mass of pines
Is such as must always exist. My straight
Route to Carolina Builders leaves out of account
Those leaves in peripheral vision, which hold
Their benediction just beyond focus.
I envy dead farmers their roofs, their rust:
At home in these spaces. Ripples
Of motion where a dove alighted
Undulate in meadows like seacoast breakers.

Friday afternoon, the house going well,
My contractor and I surrender:
Unmatchable beauty of mountain laurel,
Accumulated atmospheres, farmhouses' shaded-over wells.
We drive Orange County's backcountry,
Getting drunk in a red Ford pickup,
See a golden eagle rising high,
Over almost the spot where his bootlegging father
Hid the still in a chicken house.
The hundred dollar bills
He remembers on the kitchen table
Blew away like leaves when Pa died of cancer.
We look through an honorable old house
By the river, windows broken out
Under eighty-year oaks.
Kicking at beer cans, I see that our families
Leave headstones for legacies.
Why try to homestead an undertow of grass?

Maybe our misery gives that finishing perspective,
As when barns hold hills like a varnished canvas.
Atmosphere gathers to the wells of these yards,
Most breathlessly recedes
Where a house-corner cuts it:
Canopied by oaks, suspended on distance.

Roadside Notes in Ragged Hand

Meeting her has torn me open to feel everything again

oak leaves broken to fists by winter, still clinging branches,
        that crunch into my feelings like pebbles
I have in my chest the hidden water running like song
        birds quick-hidden where the brush piles:
                                berries on a spray

I think of my wife without guilt
                yet landscape of so many emotions
yet wear of the time and distance between us
my flesh hill-edge clay rusting to gullies.

Plenty of buzzards this blue day
        balancing on windy edges the clouds make
four wooden cows far on a hillslope
        as if a very small hand had set them there

buzzards tentative and rocking
        handling with upbent feathers at wingtip edges
currents bulking up into sky
big as watertank-towering pines, boulders which fat
the clouds irregular cheeks
                        it is love I think
which likens these four things together
        the bird the cloud the tree the stone
without it rivers would not run
                and all things break apart to dissimilitude.

Halfway home I remember first love with my wife
        gullies with grass in any country
remind me of then, cave with a skein
which fates my wandering always
                    engaging manhood

now as I approach home broomstraw is moving
satiate with winter light on all fields around me
        the last stretch of road I take is dirt
clay trail red as flesh, cobbled with many rocks like buds of a tongue.

Water

Downward in direction as a willow,
        white rapids flowering in your hair,
O life-and-death lingering
        and beginning, element of Ophelia:

your communities are rotifers
        churning; puddles cupped in stumps
round the womb-sacs of insects,
        hold daphnia, flutters of cilia—

yet you are an expanding glitter,
        wind scaling bronze across a river,
are puddles with pollen and frogs
        where mud bubbles the noise rejoice.

O pattered-down patterning,
        prefiguring of spray upon a bough,
you are liquid for spring's generation,
        for tadpole sperm to gather in.

Your molecules link into chains
        slippery for the capillary thirst,
which trees satisfy, defying gravity,
        though entropy drains you toward the sea.

Material spirit, vapor in breath,
        gauze for our entrance and exits,
you sheathe our wet begetting,
        are breathed out finally at death.

You always are single yet double:
        where oxygen triangles, the one
between two, with androgynous hydrogen,
        a woman bends supple.

Blood Ties: For Jan

In the forty-nine Ford I had earned,
We printed our tires
Into dirt below our special tree.
Ascending on wings
Of insects and leaves, we flew
In a slippage that was tight
And all freedom
On a wind above
Corn in the dark.

Our blood in an updraft column
Lifted off
In a suspended moment
Out of touch with the earth
As if endless
Like a fountain evanescent under lights
Till it burst
Toward the stars
Like our bonfire sparks at night

And then drifting
Winking out
Until lightning bugs hovering
In a honeysuckle odor
When we raised our heads to the window again
Were scattered over fields
Like embers of burning
As if we'd seeded the air with our fire.

Our bodies retreated,
Blood flowing west toward the long-gone sun.
We lay back happy
But hushed, mute, and grave,
Afraid of the permanence of the love we had made,
Afraid of our knowledge: two after Eden.

Pamlico River

I breathed that odor of land-draining water,
Leachings from ditches and saw-bladed marshes,
From springs, field-trickles, now channeled by creeks
Into a five-mile flood turned bronze in the sun:
Cypresses ever in the distances, living
And dead, fish hawks nesting their skeletons.
I breathed that odor of ending and beginning,
Land's drift marrying with salt and the tides.
I lay on a spit of sand in the sun,
Savoring the taste of my body and water.
My cousin Ethel cooked steaks on a fire,
Ethel's beau and I sipped beer. That spirit
From childhood, whose cloud-imagination
Trailed the rain in necklaces, felt winelike
Arteries and veins, intoxicating stems,
Like grandfather's scuppernong: grapes in leaves
Grown yellow with October too sweet to resist.

January Farmhouse

Snow on ground and
Brown weeds above: patches
Like fragments of dinner plate
Where sun brushes clay.
The washboard wall is in shadow,
Holds skim milk light
The way a bedsheet hung out to dry
And catch cold's cleanliness
Gathers sheen from the sky.
The white boards appear
Translucent, like a woman's skin
When she is old and left alone
The January afternoon;
Seem translucent with enclosing
Light I see through an upstairs window
Collected in a dresser mirror;
Or see from glimpsing
Through front and back windows,
All the way through those rooms,
Through this still afternoon
In her life and back into sky,
Where sun slants clearly
Without clay, or broom sedge,
Or skin to make rosy, there
Where wind's too thin to be seen.

White Lake

Rimmed in by cypresses, tin water flashed
Like the top of a can, in fields still buzzing
With cicadas: electrical August short-circuiting.
The surface slicked over us like oil, shone
Silver with clouds. We walked, holding hands,
Toward the rides: Roller Coaster. Dive Bomber.
We sat in the Ferris wheel, throbbing
With its engine, as it hurried us backward,
To show a black polish, the lake like marble
Under stars, bulbs on its opposite shore
Rolling across reflection in miniature pearls.

With a wince of thrill in the quick of our spines,
We offered up ourselves to a turning as enormous
As the seasons or desire, whirled down to search
Shadows, where water lapped subtly at roots,
For a place we could lie down together, wandered
Through glare from the lighted piers,
Till we took our chances below a capsized boat.
In the rides park afterward, there were dolls
To be won by rings or thrown balls.
Formal in black and white, pandas
Like drunken guests at a wedding faced
A tree-tall whirling as if spun by a giant.

Firewood

After the axe head has flashed
And the maple log is sawed,
He lingers on the hearth,
Anticipating light, for this sun

In wood is somehow in his blood,
As his eyes flicker clearly
Their spark in the thicket
Of a world not understood.

It is not only a golden
Living descended to timber
That the child's struck match
Frees to dancing,

There are October's odors
Veined into foliage, which a boy
And his man of flame
Exhale as smoke to the cold.

This story he thinks, a blond
Prince lost in a forest,
Is as tragic and old
As a chemical formula.

Not only fire descended
To water and fiber, but wonder
At the union he senses,
That to living antennas

Of branches, sun should
Signal through the clearness,
To maple leaves and apples,
Coloring with sugar,

For a meeting more than either.
He senses how flame returned
From leaves toward sun
Musks air with mortal October.

Some Words for Fall

The tobacco's long put in. Whiffs of it curing
Are a memory that rustles the sweet gums.
Pete and Joe paid out, maybe two weeks ago.
The way their hard hands hook a bottle of Pepsi Cola,
It always makes me lonesome for something more.
The language they speak is things to eat.
Barbecue's smell shines blue in the wind.
Titles of Nehi Grape, Dr Pepper, are nailed
Onto barns, into wood sides silvered and alive,
Like the color pork turns in heat over ashes.

I wish I could step through the horizon's frame
Into a hand-hewn dirt-floored room.
People down home in Eastern N.C.,
When they have that unlimited longing,
They smell the packhouse leavings.
They look at leaves like red enamel paint
On soft drink signs by the side of the road
That drunks in desperation have shot full of holes.
No words they have are enough.
Sky in rags between riverbank trees
Pieces the torn banner of heroic *name*.

From as Far Away as Dying

And now in the end I see this community together,
Under angles of poor wooden gables and porches,
Accumulated in vision and fronting the west at evening,
With figures fixed in humblest gesture, descending
A warped step, arising from porch swing or rocker,
Or stooping to spit tobacco, become an architectural face
Above Salisbury's entrance, man and wife, their cotton turned
Rosy by sun, as if King at Wells with elbows
Thrust from his throne, or stone-wimpled Lady medievally
Distant, in that air I remember, like choirs of all souls:
Beside posts, porch railings—voices, this saintly communion.

The Mary Tapes

I

Mary Woods was my name, before I married
A Hill. The recorder was Roger's present,
So now I've got to think what to say.
My mind is on the house we're building,
And Raleigh seems so far from our town down home,
I feel like I've moved to a different century.
But those first days don't leave you. I remember
Living there, in a tenant shack out behind grandma's.
Sun made the roof tin creak like a stove
Cooling off; our hall felt rickety, pine boards
That bounced you up and down when you walked.
Near the kitchen stove, where the linoleum ended,
I could see white flashings through the cracks,
When our chickens ran underneath the floor.

I'm halfway embarrassed to hear myself talk,
When it comes back out so flat and country.
I can manage their English well enough—
Yes, my dear, I see your point perfectly.
But the way you talk when you're being *correct*
Won't let my aching get eased into words.
This loneliness catches in my throat,
And tears seem beading like a sweat inside.
Their regular words go numb and deadly.
When I try to think of who I really am,
I see a circle of water in a mason jar.
I'm carrying it to daddy, where he's plowing tobacco.
Dirt through the toes of my sandals feels powdery
And hot, like wood ashes shoveled from the stove.
It seems old-timey, with daddy in the field,
And him and the mule kind of small and so lost
In the corner by the river, where trees billow up
High as a cliff, and thunderheads are piled even higher,
Like an avalanche ready to bury us in whiteness.

Listening to a mourning dove call, I'd forget
What I was doing, like I had lost my own name.
My eyes might as well have been from
Somebody dead, a woman out of one of those yellow
Tin pictures, her dress draped around her like curtains.
A sadness would be running with the river from horses,
That crippled up their riders, or carried them to battle.
And the water would be sliding inside a smell
Like a skin, snaking away the sunshine.
What I was lonesome for felt close by then.
My great-great-grandparents and aunts and uncles
Were there in that field but hidden out of sight,
And the ones who were swept away and drowned
When they tried to cross the ford in high water
Were still in a stream running underneath the river.

People can't ever be happy. The folks
Down home were ignorant and ill as rattlesnakes.
Families would quarrel, or talk would start
About a woman and the preacher, till her husband
Had his shotgun out, with his eyes like he'd drunk
From a kerosene lantern and was about to catch fire.
I have to remember the loneliness and meanness,
Along with the feelings of forever. We'd swim
In a pond, and come up with water on our lashes,
So the bushes and grass would look early with dew,
Like drying off from just being made.
I didn't feel then like I ever could die,
Or bad things ever could happen. The way
That air felt in the fields, like biting an apple,
Was everything I wanted. Having Jimmy scared me,
But it was the sadness later that changed my feelings.
Jimmy was just a baby in his crib.
I'd walked up the road, to see if there was mail.
When I came back in, he was blue and still.
The covers were not over his face or anything.
It near about killed me. I cried for a week

Like I was crazy. I wouldn't eat meals
Or look in people's faces, just sat with my fingers
Kind of messed up in tears and in my hair.
I found out later that crib deaths happen.
I took it on my own self then.
The one thing that saved our marriage, was Roger
Never said even the least little word to blame me.

I couldn't stand snakes run over on the pavement,
Or frogs squashed flat to little skins.
It worried me when wind piled high in the clouds,
And swooshed against our house with rain in a river.
Lightning looked as crooked as Satan's pitchfork.
Everything that was dirty and evil seemed
Hopping and crawling out of bushes and ditches
When storms were making veils on the fields.
I was the one who had let it all happen,
Had let Roger get in between my legs
When we were still in high school, parked on
The ox road at night, when honeysuckle breaths
From the ditches would tangle inside with our panting.
That was why Jimmy had died, I imagined.
So we sold our little piece of the farm,
And Roger went to school at N.C. State.

Here in the Piedmont, you don't feel so ignorant
And doomed, with planes taking off for New York,
And hospitals and doctors if the kids get sick.
Ginger and Cindy are seven and nine,
And I'm thirty-seven. Now we've decided
We like the country after all. The land
Up here isn't scary, with its rolling hills;
The sky doesn't crowd so close at the horizon.
Some radio tower or T.V. antenna
Is poking up there in the distance, and the trees
Don't look too powerful, so you love them better.
I especially like falls, with daisies and chicory

By the road, and sweet gums turning their different colors.
Magazines like *Better Homes and Gardens*
Gave me a lot of ideas for our house.
Our lot is in a woodsy new section,
With a stream over rocks along the back.
A drawing of just the right roof for the place
Will shine in my head, the rafters raised up
Like sunbeams, marking out a space in the trees.
The plan we're building is near 'bout like that.
Our stream has pools that are clear to the bottom,
With minnows there fanning tame as goldfish,
And leaves crumpled up on the surface, drifting
With the wind, like not really touching the water.
Trees on our lot will be fresh as the woods
Down home, but with briars cleaned out, and poison
Ivy vines cut from next to the rocks.
Our furniture, and books in their glass-fronted cases,
Will make our rooms look bright like a picture,
So shadow from a crow passing over, or a snake,
Can't make us feel gloomy enough to die.

II

Putting in tobacco, I'd laugh with the others,
But sometimes I'd feel uneasy, my bosoms
Little budding-up things, like halves of green apples.
The woman named Nank, who helped us, was quick
As a mink, could strike out dangerous as a moccasin.
The razor blade between her two fingers
Had already cut you when you saw it.
Her Indian cheekbones made her eyes look squinty.
Field niggers leaned in the packhouse door
Where she was grading at the table. It gave me
Goose bumps, she looked so womanly dangerous,
Her bosoms in that shirt showing deep between.
The dust looked brassy in sun through the door,
Like the summer stored up. The hand wanting Nank

Was afraid to be sassy, he knew she'd cut him
Like a cold wind had carried a razor.
Her eyes looked as black as two buttons,
And after he was gone, a sick-feeling
Wonder and longing was left in my stomach.
Nank would tickle so it hurt my bosoms
And ask me if boys had ever done it to me.
I felt all flushed like hot water inside.
Grown-ups' secrets could cramp you like colic.
When a woman at the revival got crazy
With Jesus, and her lips turned back,
Like grinning and hurting at one time,
I imagined how her loving must have felt.

Things seem more reasonable here in the Piedmont.
So when Roger got a mind to chase tail, I didn't
Let it feel like the end of the world,
Like people down home, when they'd kill somebody.
We met this doctor and his wife at a party,
And he was a pretty-faced man, the kind
Whose wife is real plain, about as good-looking
As he might be, with a wig and some powder.
So anyway I made up this complaint, with heart
Palpitations, and dizziness when I first stood up.
The appointments were set in the late afternoons,
And after I got out, I'd shop, or drive around.
Roger looked worried when I got home
One evening after nine. I asked him
If the kids had had supper. He said they all
Went to Hardee's, when I didn't come back.
The appointments were all late, I said.
His pupils looked dark and as big as an owl's.
He asked me to tell if that doctor was
"Abusing my trust." I laughed in his face.
I wasn't Snow White, or his daughter, I said.
If he wanted to be chasing some narrow-assed girl,
Who just barely knew enough to type,

Don't talk to me about some sacred trust.
And if he had a taste for new dishes,
Maybe I would eat out myself.
He grabbed me right rough by the shoulders,
And shook me so the hair fell in my face,
And my hand got loose by itself and slapped him,
And he caught me by the throat, with his eyes
Like they were staring into too-bright sun,
And didn't even see me. I asked if he loved me,
Because the folks down home used to kill ones
They loved. His face changed quick, like a cloud
Before the sun. We sat down trembling,
And talked it out, and afterwards made love.
I'd wanted to get away from all that,
But took after my folks enough, I guess,
To have to have a love-fight with Roger.
I can't blame them too much, remembering
What we came up from. Daddy got started
With wiring work during World War Two,
On a hangar for blimps in Elizabeth City.
Later he climbed poles in the middle of the country,
And worked up to be the superintendent
Of a whole town's lights and water.
You think we weren't proud, in our shiny Buick,
Driving down the main street at night, when store windows
And cars looked kind of famous with lights,
When my daddy was the one in charge of the current.

What brought this up was the luck we had
With our lot. The power company did it.
We went out there on a Sunday and they'd cut
This right-of-way from next to the creek.
Their tarry light poles, lying around, looked as rusty
As cannons. The trees were chain-sawed down
So it reminded me of pictures of Civil War battlefields,
People piled up with their shirts blown open.
The stream looked naked in the sun, like some

Young girl that they'd pulled the clothes off of.
Roger really loves me, I guess. His face got
Tender when I kept on sitting on that pine log
With catches hiccupping in my breathing, as if the girl
Who had heard daddy's linemen "mother fucking,"
And their joking sneakiness like greasy mechanics,
Like their hands would smear you in patches like bruises
Wherever they touched, was still inside.
I was talking crazy, said the men fought battles
And tore up cornfields and trees and came home
One-armed and heroic from whichever war
And let women do the worrying. But Roger said
We had us a peace from the old destruction.
He got that real estate man on the phone,
And told him how the woods had been ruined.
That salesman got his mess to the development
And saved the last lot from being cut.
We're going to break ground tomorrow. I dread
That red clay mud, and the two-by-fours
With nails sticking through, and the leftover
Bags of cement that get hard in the rain,
But some things you have to have to live.
The clotted-up lumps can remind me of folks
Down home, their faces as purple as brickbats,
When they died with a stroke. Me and Roger
Will remember, we've lived through too much now,
With Jimmy and the other little house and the plans
For this one, with changing the front door,
And what kind of linoleum to buy,
And agreeing on fixtures for the front-porch light.
We've kept love together this far.
I know I see windows where the trees are now.
There must be a light in the evenings out there
To brighten up our lives in one place.
Sometime it has to come as clear as I've dreamed.

IV

Iron Age Flying

I

What's the red light? Oh Boarding Boarding.
I'm walking down a ramp into a tunnel.
Jesus, it's raining. Top of the plane
Seems a wet slick whale's back.
Jonah to England, with my sins
All upon me.
Why does it feel so like dying?
Riding the river in the speedboat with father,
I didn't feel fearful.
I wasn't so personal.
A kid's just anyone,
One drop of light into the sun's bright water.

Inside it's a cave.
Maybe find a seat by a window.
Important personalities are Cadillacs.
Black shams, limousines
Appropriate for funerals. The child soul inside.
How do you believe in this idiotic century?
I wasn't inventing the things I remembered.
Father as if mowing the evening,
The light in particles of dust
But they were shining.
Seatbelt. Good, we're moving.
Faster and faster. Like rising
Toward heaven. Is this how it will be?
Regret and desire. Memories.
The red fire jumping as if speaking in tongues.
He drove away the tanker for our lives, through
The gasoline sea of her fear.

My neck feels cramped. What time
Could it be? Must have been asleep.
Move the pillow from the window.
And *where* could we be?

With lights down below.
A city. A galaxy.
Beautiful with distance and darkness.
Perhaps my life,
If seen from that remove —
With irregular beads, it becomes a necklace
Stringing a peninsula —
Are there rocks by the lights and black-foil water?
It's a bay within the land's last arms.

II

We are going and we have been:
To climb along the Somerset headlands
Resurrected from an underground England.
We'll scramble clay holes through
Iron age forts — no stones of Camelot —
Considering the blades from Saxon barrows.

Iron age, hand
In a rusty glove, handle
My throat, my thoughts,
Gently.

I began with a boy, whose sight
Was marked by a snake.
Though his brown time drains
With the Pamlico River,
Everything seen in his life
Flows in an underground stream
Where a new sun burns.

Over our horizon to the east, the constant
Night of Earth's own shadow
Is a cone standing still,
So that children, animals, weeds, and jewels
Spin through it, where a vision
Lies buried

Like treasure: one gleaming
Bearing the world revolves on,
Earth-lidded eyeball, wink of the Cyclops.
Underground sun, give us prospect
On our landscape's mud, our poor map of paths
Which spin, recombine, in the head,
Like threads dyed red
From real sheepfolds,
To stitch incorrigible imagination's pastoral.

Iron age flying, over
The planet's body where dawn still hides,
Telescope fields: the contours
Planted with a garden not realized.
Egg of earth holds the sun inside.

English Church Towers

The farther you walk away from them, the higher
They aspire across the intervening buildings:
Not dream-riotous gargoyles leering from moldings,
But divine dumb beasts from elsewhere, foreheads on fire
With spires of idea, limestone shells mooring reluctantly in air
Bodies like tortoises' grown to ornamented bone.
Our weather surprises these animals from different skies.
As a horse in sun-blind pasturage is perplexed by flies,
They are sucked and bitten by bills of lichen, pierced by frost.
The bells they sound breed moth-like moments, swarming as if to snuff
Some flame. Minute bites minute by minute for long enough
Will teach their stone the mortality we suffer.
Their countenanced towers decay like ours, though slower.
There's something in us that sculptures angels in glory,
Then forgets them in rain, half-wingless, sooty
Among vines and tombslabs. Not revenge upon the eternal, exactly.
But this spark of ourselves, we acquaint with its damp counterpart.
We wished down Christ to Madonna among us, for his spread-wing
Pelican death on a stake. Could then restore

Him with his mother, and adore them, in scarlet and azure
Glass, earth-brown Calvaries horizoning to gold, canopies
With a holy fire permanently aspiring:
Heavens leaded to iconoclastic centuries.

Evening in Bath

The chandelier was crystal in the Royal Crescent Hotel.
Flies, to piped music, wove a minuet in miniature.
I bent formal elbows to feed, considering whether hell
Might be dining alone without end, windowed from nature.
No, that was melodramatic posturing. Wiltshire to Devon
Seemed drying and dying about my grant's numbered route.
Drought and the loneliness were what had me low. The Avon
At Bradford was suffocating its picturesque trout.
I'd watched one curve up its side, under elms gone brown,
Like hedgerows dead by the motorway, parched by cars.
England, I know, will be many mild years going down,
Yet the Royal Hospital's veterans, no imperial wars
Having lately been fought, age on feebler and fewer,
And I am moved unreasonably by English mums and children,
Missing my own, I suppose. To know it will be no better
For their uniformed offspring should sober the English men.

In face of the Roman, Saxon, Norman, Elizabethan, Restoration,
Hanoverian stone, no policy or party centers blame.
Invaders came, things caught fire. Bombs fell, later on.
The abbeys and minsters, if so much as a wall and a name
Remained, would be built up again. Ralph Allen's house
Above Bath still weaves upon vacant space a symphony
Of urns, as the observer changes his place. Can rouse,
Within pitted stone, a more vivid, self-assured century.

For bejeweled old birds shared the dining room at dinner.
A daughter seemed ancient as mother. One had had Dubonnet
Before, wishing for a Conservative prime minister.
She fluttered her nails at inflation, hoped we'd not let
Blacks marry whites in the States. A garden out back
Was my refuge, until the porter's cat came over the wall
With a finch he'd caught, formal in his full dress of black.
He tossed it by the law of his nature, narrow-eyed, implacable.

Royal Hospital

The Royal Hospital's pensioners
Are veterans of no recent wars.
Within iron-old gates, prisoners,
They sit mildly, where flowers
Trim gravel, at ease in uniforms
Like those of firemen, second children
Awaiting some play of drums.
Before buildings by Christopher Wren,
Eighteenth-century bronze mute
Muzzles stand ready to repel whatever
Can be repelled by the Queen's salute.
There are playing fields toward the river,
But no young bodies to volley
Or bowl as at martial Eton.
The brown, barged Thames looks empty
Under the arc in keeping of these cannon.
Pensioners tend foxglove, grave
And memorial, their garden like colors
Of ribbon which mark the degrees brave
They shone in their youth, when others

In the battle lay dying or dead.
Empire and warfare is a ceremonial
Music faintly far from overhead,
While these remember, and that is all.

Beginning with Egypt

(The British Museum)

Manuscript and mummy, awl, gold, bowl and skull:
A detritus of civilizations. Clay-breasted mother,
Your face was a blade or a beak then, perfunctory pinch
By his fingers, whose dream filled those thighs' cornucopia.
Your Old Kingdom milky breasts were Isis. Long before
Madonnas, you suckled Horus. Violent pot full
Of tillage and births—between bestial Bes, a dwarf,
And Min with erection as long as three thousand years—
Your seed cram us still into stretch-belly time.

In a later niche, by crouching Aphrodite, I give thanks
To the inventors of loveliness: there is clear-faced Demeter,
These Aurorae with stone gauze of wind between the knees.
An artist's folds envelop those thighs in their mystery,
Whose sweet fat in stone erupts the shape of the Divine.

Foreseeing the Journey

The fan inhales one continuous breath: through
This upstairs room I am lying awake in, foreseeing the journey.
This creek, this street, this one row of houses, diagram Town.
As simple as the world. As air and the light. Old birthplace.
Tomorrow we'll go with the current, canoe around snags—
As I guide my son through the thicket of childhood—
Past moccasins uglier than the Biblical serpent.
Passion-flowers as in Rousseau's jungles.

This four-bladed beating, as of great hawks crossed,
Sucks moths from their flight, with light's
Exhalation, draws foil-glint wings from the corn.
Its rumble surrounds me. Our bungalow lifts off, zeppelin
With roof, shadow more angled than a biplane bomber.
I seem Huck Finn visiting a house on the flood.
Books from around me hover their pages. With Zane Grey
And Edgar Rice Burroughs, presents bobbing up like helium
In the attic—my Christmas models in a loose formation—
I fly in the flock of these presences, owls with the heads

Of dead relatives, the photograph of my mother's brothers
Sailing in the ghost wind, until the huge cry they feel
Becomes one with the wailing of the fan,
This rest what I can do and no more fear.

Almon who told me the Cyclops' blinding
Looks so beautiful there, delicate of feature, shy
With sister, ignorant of the years of high school teaching,
The loneliness to come. But not consumed
By my mother's weeping, for all who have died,
Her father Mercer's fall under his buggy,
I fly in this house and its history
As in Lord Greystoke's plane above the trees.
Would any of us be born into the world
If we had it to do over?
Through this sleep of the unborn and of spirits
The propeller tom-toms a message.

The attic fan in this window, ill-designed,
Dangerous, great blades unshielded, drive belt
Exposed to the unwary night walker,
Put in by my father in jack-leg fashion
Like everything down east, by him who lost
His fingers to an air compressor belt,
Seems the risk of all living. I'm flying too high
But in the dawn light chill I reach down
To find a blanket green as leaves.
I pull up the jungle over my body.

V

Jonquils

At the ruined homestead in spring,
Where armatures of honeysuckle,
Baskets of weed-wire, sprawl over
Old rows, twine up fruit trees,
Where poison oak thicker than adders chokes about
Stones of a hearth—a broken altar—
The jonquils have risen. Their yellows gather
On sea-colored stems. The frilled bells
Face in all directions, with a scattering of general
Attention toward the sun: now gone, yet source
Of their butter, their gold, this lidded day—
As if sunlight broken in pieces were
Rising from the earth. Like
Bright women abandoned in the wilderness.

Collards

Green hens perching the pole
        Of a row, concentric wings
Fly you down into soil.

You catch the rain like rings
        Where a pine stump tunnels
Time backward down roots' seasonings.

Beside roots' dark channels
        Mining the forest, your fiber
Threads grease in the entrails

Of families, whose bodies harbor
        Scars like rain on a hillslope,
Whose skin takes the sheen of lumber

Left out in the weather. Old folk
        Seem sewed together by pulp
Of your green rope and smoke

From the cook fires boys gulp
        For dinner along roads in winter.
Collards and the ham grease they drop

In a pot come back as we enter
        The house with porch and a pumpkin.
This steam holds all we remember.

Sweet potatoes clot in a bin,
        Common flesh beneath this skin
Like collards. Grainy-sweet, kin.

A Leaf of Tobacco

Is veined with mulatto hands. The ridges extending
Along crests of the topographical map from the stem
Marking a mountainous ridge encounter wrinkles
Where streams lead down toward coastal pocosins.
This time-yellowed scrap of a partial history
Features humans driven on like mules with no reprisal.
The grit your fingers feel exploring this pungent terrain
Is fragments of a Staffordshire tea service
Buried from Sherman in fields near Bentonville.
The snuff-colored resin on the ball of your finger
Crystallized in the corners of seventy-five-year-old lips,
On the porch of a shotgun shack, as she watched her grandsons
Crop lugs on their knees in the sun. This leaf has collected,
Like a river system draining a whole basin,
The white organdy lead bullet coon dog Baptist
Preacher iron plow freed slave raped and
Bleeding dead from the lynch mob cotton
Mouth South. Scented and sweetened with rum and molasses,
Rolled into cigarettes or squared in a thick plug,
Then inhaled or chewed, this history is like syrupy
Moonshine distilled through a car radiator so the salts
Strike you blind. Saliva starts in the body. We die for this leaf.

Barbecue Service

I have sought the elusive aroma
Around outlying cornfields, turned corners
Near the site of a Civil War surrender.
The transformation may take place
At a pit no wider than a grave,
Behind a single family's barn.
These weathered ministers
Preside with the simplest of elements:
Vinegar and pepper, split pig and fire.
Underneath a glistening mountain in air,
Something is converted to a savor: the pig
Flesh purified by far atmosphere.
Like the slick-sided sensation from last summer,
A fish pulled quick from a creek
By a boy. Like breasts in a motel
With whiskey and twilight
Become a blue smoke in memory.
This smolder draws the soul of our longing.

I want to see all the old home folks,
Ones who may not last another year.
We will rock on porches like chapels
And not say anything, their faces
Impenetrable as different barks of trees.
After the brother who drank has been buried,
The graveplot stunned by sun
In the woods,
We men still living pass the bottle.
We barbecue pigs.
The tin-roofed sheds with embers
Are smoking their blue sacrifice
Across Carolina.

Southern Voices

If you understand my accent,
You will know it is not out of ignorance.
Broom sedge in wind has curved this bent
Into speech. This clay of vowels, this diffidence

Of consonantal endings, murmurs *defeat*:
Caught like a chorus from family and servants.
This is the hum of blessings over the meat
Your cavalry spared us, echoed from an aunt's

Bleak pantry. This colorless tone, like flour
Patted onto the cheeks, is poor-white powder
To disguise the minstrel syllables lower
In our register, from a brownface river.

If it sounds as if minds were starved,
Maybe fatback and beans, yams and collards
Weighed down vitamins of wit, lard
Mired speed, left wetlip dullards

In cabins by cotton. But if bereft
Of the dollars and numbers, our land's whole
Breath stirs with its Indian rivers. Our cleft
Palate waters for a smoke of the soul,

A pungence of pig the slaves learned
To burn in pits by the levee. This melon
Round of field and farmer, servant turned
Tenant, longs for a clear pronunciation,

But stutters the names of governors, Klan
And cross-burnings, mad dogs and lynchings.
So ours is the effacing slur of men
Ashamed to speak. We suffer dumb drenchings

Of honeysuckle odor, love for a brother
Race which below the skin is us, lust
Projected past ego onto this shadow-other.
So we are tongue-tied, divided, the first

To admit face to face our negligence
And ignorance of self: our musical tone
Of soul-syllable, penchant for the past tense,
Harelip contractions unable to be one.

The Morning After

As our President sleeps I see (in the dream
He cannot remember) industrial suburbs.
Petrochemical refineries isolate themselves in a glamour
Of lights by the Delaware, the James, the Savannah rivers.
Fumes fly like flags from catalytic towers.
Burnt stumps, half-extracted, rim strip mine cavities.
Hard-hat men watch bulldozers consuming pastures,
Streams run mud like the aftermath of Gettysburg.
The meaning of this carnage of flattening and poisoning
Is these blocks with the family grocery closing,
These thin card houses to be swept away
And set up again by the car-blast of freeways.
The meaning of this sacrifice of clear running
Drink without metallic pollutants is the trail bike
For eleven year old boys, the reverberation
Of lawnmower engines against the brick walls
Of disused schools. The meaning of this poisoning
And dulling of the land is a poisoning and
Dulling of the mind, a satiety with televised
Violence and beer, a dull stupor of
Desire for desire like lava-colored underground
Coal fires eating their way toward our children.
Undetermined substances leach deeper into Love Canal.
The outgoing tide leaves mud flats mounded
With feces, dead birds coated with oil.
He smiles, asleep, his expression comforts,
He mouths unconsciously the names of our
Accomplishments, athletes and astronauts
Chewed with the bodies of Marines and underfed
Children in a saliva striped like the flag.

Greene County Pastoral

I hope that Mary Alice Philips who lived
      by the river will pick new
            jonquils for the casket.

Maybe L. G. Newcomb whose four-room house
      stood in a bend of the creek road
            will come with a fist of forsythia.

I wish the girls and boys I knew, from creekside and
      mule lot, from rosy broom sedge knolls,
            could start past edges of pine woods.

I think their singing and sighing might rustle
      with the needles and hush like the dove
            wings alighting on light wires

On hills far away in the country. Their preachers
      might come looking pale and fresh-shaven
            from the white inside the wooden churches.

May their sermons on sin and punishment subside,
      let them calm those waters. Let Jesus walk
            out of their words and pass among

L. G.'s crowd where they're turning the reel in the Contentnea.
      Let his face be from faces in the boats on
            the Neuse, the Pamlico, the Cape Fear.

Those who drowned, let them arise.
      The white face of one from underwater
            will still these troubles. While they

Scoop up nets full of shad and cats and their
      campfire flickers more orange as the sun
            goes down, may the mules

In the fenced lots hang their heads sorrowfully
        and turn their hindquarters to the wind,
            one hoof scraping a corn cob.

May wind through dog fennel of the deserted
        pasture sway the soft weeds just at the tips
            so they touch the fence's wire.

May the sky and the land be one in evening,
        the pale light a lake for the straw
            and the twigs and the weeds

And fish in the reel and the horses and mules
        and Mary Alice Philips and L. G.,
            and Christ like a drowned man arisen.

Let the deserted house with scrolled cornices
        in the grove of broken oaks with a few
            jonquils spotting that shadow

Be circled like an elegy by swallows.
        Let them know that she always loved them.
            Let this light and these fields

Hold her spirit as naturally as a straw
        basket carries the loose flowers.
            Let the light in that cloud fade to stone.

May she lie at peace with the forsythia, spirea, willow
        brought her by bare-footed farm girls
            in my frail thoughts' pastoral.

Quitting Time

Mill workers migrating
north with the four
o'clock shift from
American Tobacco
stream the road,
refugees, battered big
Plymouths and Olds
hiding rust and dirt under
pretentious fenders:
sliding and nosing toward
Roses and K-Mart toward
collards and ham hock and
a cotton tee shirt,
a beer before T.V. —
toward a cigarette's
blue ghost and ash and
forgetfulness or argument.
Even asleep, life is
sweet. Imaginations sullen
with poverty and illness
are still imaginations. The third
finger slips into the
elastic fissure. Spring
brings zinnias to the
garden. Though refugees of
mental fight surrendered
unconditionally, they are
quilted against the cold
by polyester. If whoever stole
imagination's wealth
would give it back —
give red and gold
thread — their fingers
would embroider.

How to Fix a Pig

(as told by Dee Grimes)

Take a piece of tin that's
Blowed off a barn in a storm.
Pile little limbs and good chunks
Of hickory on top. Get the fire going
While you're finishing the pit.
Hickory burns orange, then blue.
Dig deep enough to hide a flat-bottomed
Creek boat. Put bars across the top
Closer together then the ones in a jail.
Flop the split pig skin side down
So his eyes won't watch you.
Take a little hit from the bottle in your pocket.
When you've got good coals,
Spread 'em out under him with
A flat-ended shovel. Pretty soon
The steam starts. Douse on the vinegar
And pepper. First time you sniff him,
You start to get hungry. But you can't rush a pig.
Eat that cold chunk of corn bread
You brought from the house in a greasy paper bag.
When that vinegar and wood ashes smoke starts rising,
And blowing in a blue wind over fields,
It seems like even the broom straw
Would get hungry. But you got to stand it
At first. It comes from down home,
When they cured tobacco with wood, and ears of corn
Roasted in ashes in the flue.
The pig was the last thing. The party
At the looping shelter, when the crop was all in.
The fall was in its smell,
Like red leaves and money.
So when you can't stand it, turn up the rib side.

If you didn't get started before light,
You may be finishing after dark.

The last sparks look at you red from underneath,
Like the pig's eyes turned into coals, but forgiving.
When the whole thing's finally so brown
And tender it near 'bout
Falls to pieces when you move it,
Slide it every bit into the pan.
They're waiting to chop it up at the house.
And they going to wonder one more time
Why a pig don't have no ribs when it's done.

The Advisors

Throned on the piled treads, tired,
I'd sit like a prince with his advisors,
Orange drink for sundown. What a cast of characters.
Bill Davis damned if he'd take any shit
Since the war, when he'd carried a BAR.
And him the lightest man in his whole unit.
Ralph, ex-Marine, washing hands in gasoline.
Rabbit-toothed James with his country guitar.

With grease guns on fittings, we fired.
We broke loose the bead from truck tire rim
With wedges pounded in. Our hired
Hands felt the pressure hose heave
When blasting country mud from underneath fenders.
With kerosene stinging our skin, the spanners
Too hot to handle, we sighed for night, when we were free.
One girl was never enough, if they were me.

Ralph had fed his black market Scotch
One more time to the Australian nurse,
Who wouldn't come across. Then Alice
Drove up for gas, and Ralph polished glass
Over her dress back almost to her crotch
So I wobbled with laughter on my column of rubber.
As couples in pairs drifted to Rooster's for beer,
I weighed father's coins in my pocket, felt myself heir.

Counselors who'd spent their time, they knew
Better now. The thing was to know that I was rich.
My father owned the station. If I got an itch. . . .
You could have gone off just then I said.
Shit boy. You don't know my Jen. When you're married. . . .
I saw the American heads on a path in New Guinea.
The Japs, Ralph said, had stuck their dicks in their mouths.
Time flies, he said. Look at these moths.

Bill came back with a Bud, hair still wet. I been
Meaning to ask, I said. Ever get it in
With the teacher in the girdle? Yeah. Funny
Thing is, he said, there on my knees with a hard on
Is what I remember. See before I go to sleep.
He yawned and left, while I was closing up.
I rolled home each rubber round of that throne,
Both hands shepherding treads. Flock of black sheep.

VI

World's Shoulder, Turning

A rock with the bulk of a house leaned out
From bank across the creek — as if earth were still
In the making. Through the weed screen, I noticed
How light had lessened, mountain laurel beyond
Submerged in slope-shadow. Going back, I felt white
Quartz and the bone of a bracket mushroom
Shine their beams at me. The bouquet of huckleberry
Leaves I picked seemed tiny tropical fish.
They floated on their stems as I ran, and I
Added bleached grasses like sea oats, a few
Fronds of fern. I ran lightened in the gloom
By the scarlet and tan like a torch in my hand.
Yesterday I'd seen the sun, a scoured
Copper pan, shine through pines, from a bend
Of the high shouldering trail where the horizon
Falls away. I remembered the light's raying,
Like magnetized metallic dust. I felt all
These bright things — huckleberry stems and sea oats,
Quartz rocks and mushroom — held in the field
Of sun now down below shoulder of the world's turning.

The Ford

Today the air was mist, the river full
Bank to bank with fog. The time
Grows near the birth of Christ.
Because of the solstice. Because
We see a new year like a spark
In these short, dark days. Today
I felt released by the past. I passed
The hill where ruts made by wagons
To the mill seemed Civil War breastworks.
The past was only rock from
A wall, a chimney fallen in the woodland
Of *now*. In the rain, everything
Shone green.

Crossing on Cables

I'd passed the cable crossing, thinking it too late,
Until stopped by a movement in bushes. Squirrels?
A deer? I couldn't hear more. The two-story
Boulder near the river bulked gray under
Mountain laurel. I climbed the tree that held the cables
And slid my feet over water, steadied by the strand above.

The landing led up through a staircase crevice
To a ledge giving vantage over a rippled bend.
The rock-grain felt rough as tree bark, the top
Pitted and peaked like a topographical map
Of the continent. The hundreds-of-thousands-of-years-old
Shelf shone gray-green with lichen, mossed
In spots like forests seen from space. Resting,
My hand supporting me, I felt a cold slow
Pulse pushing between my bone and the granite.

Constructing the River

The sequences of the river write themselves
Anew every day. It is a flow which dries
In lines from my pen. Fine dogwood twigs
End in periods of buds, limb-type prints
Phonemes of foam on air. Words are things.
I feel them in my brain's blood, forming with my
Running. I am accompanied through a narrowing
Where path comes close to rocky shallows by a
Continuous murmuring of the many streams' tongues
The rapids form. I use *foam, stream,* and *tongue*
For their sound. So language refers to itself.
Millipede with tail in its mouth, it circles
In these woods and every word is a leg touching
Water or tree. The cliff shows an intrusion of quartz,
Crystalline vein continuing even where
Softer stone has rotted to loam. Word is not
Object but both exist and align. This poem
I am writing is not precisely the one in my head
As I was running. This presence is an illusion.
The relation between word-thing and quartz vein
Is something seen, clear air, quintessential
As metaphor. It was not there before. Poor
As we are, this affluent gleam at the speed
Of light vibrates between noun and thing, almost
Joining them. Grandsons of Freud, we handle
The mental toy, make it disappear like mother,
Fort/da, fort/da. We visit our own funerals with
Huck Finn. The word-river cherishes time that was,
That is, that will never again be. Is elegy.

Just Rain

The steady rain grew colder as I ran.
Honeysuckle crowding across the path sopped
My shoe tops with water. The river was
Louder than ever, a continuous crescendo,
A racing flow into frothing combers.
The current's galloping took over, thought
Forced to concentrate on the path's ledge
That offered an easy slide. To go under
The tan moil and hurry with small logs
Riding it bareback seemed, to my absent
Mind, attractive. Like call of the distance
Below a precipice. Cold and uncomfortable
Rain doesn't make one's possession of self
More intense. Mind wanders to memories
Of summer, close warm smells fill the
Breath. Raw is the word for the river. I
Regretted disturbing the small birds pecking
By the ford. I lay down in weeds at
The abandoned homestead, to feel what it's
Like being dead. Rain felt pure on my face.

Tree of Babel

A green air freshened from cedar
And holly. The river's metal
Reflection shone molten.
Rocks, washed of silt,
Left the mind rinsed.
The cloth on a snag,
Like a scrap tacked to fact
From dream, was gone.
From the shore I'd crossed to by cable,
I looked back at people
Hiking on Sunday.
I waved before fading
Into trees. The boot print
I found in a clearing
(Like Friday coming on Crusoe)
Stunned me. A hundred yards on,
An ancient, forked beech
Carved with illegible
Letters seemed text
To the living story
Of abandoned rows under trees.
A scribble of vines loaded
My head like a dictionary's
Waste heap.
Beyond the written beech,
An ice-white sycamore
Spired air
With absolute moment.
I discovered the illusion
Newly. The pool of perception
Inked only by branches
Seemed garden before
Transgression, flood high over
The Babel tower. I came
Home from this year
Made new with only a happy
Headache, a thorn in my finger.

Clear Winter

Confusion of seasons is over.
Today was clear winter.
Light that on trunks seemed warm
Looked bleak and bare
On chill limbs high in chill air.
I saw bodies of trees
Piled mercilessly by past
High water, crotch-chunk
Of one upon trunk of another.
Angular cedars, their crowns
Thinned of needles by drought,
Seemed a desert tribe
Overtaken by an angel of death.
Finally I climbed clear
Of the valley which memory
Stocked with its proxy
Corpses. I saw air
In its isolation now pure.
We are unable to endure
This light the cold whets to steel.
I stood above river land
And hypothesized the being
We cannot understand, who
Begins things with flame of a star.
Who is the zero far dark.
I sniffed for scent of some smoke,
For coffee, leaf-smolder or
Cigarette odor. All unendurably
Absent. I turned toward home,
Alone as a pane of ice
The keen sun shines through.
I kissed my warm wife
And under the first star
Gathered cedar for a fire.

Like a Body in the River

The atmosphere was bitter mist—my nerves
Worse than the weather. I buttoned on
A Bean guide jacket, laced rubber foot
Boots. Running on the slushy bank felt
Childishly barefoot. I ran without thought.
A heavy plop, and circles in the river marked
A beaver I'd surprised. I stopped to watch
Its seal-like head in the sledding current,
Its outraged eye. The cocoa water grew
Darker, with bass thumps and drowning
Percussions. The river bobbled with nightmare.
Turgid screams drove at me out of my dreaming
Remembrance—like wire lines the bats
Stitched in the net of branches. I'd seen,
On a figure at a stoplight, the face
Of my friend's dead wife. Felt lost.
The sepia light rusted toward oblivion
As I groped toward home in grief.

The Sense of Light

I run in an unmoving pane
That accompanies my face, a beam
Like a stream standing still—
While vines and tree trunks flow
Furiously. Though bronze through the lens
Of sun in afternoons, this other sun
Has no tone. The father I saw,
Hovering over his toddler, will
Hold the umbrella and pull down shades
In vain. This absolute light X-rays
Walls, transparent cliff that
Crowds us to the edge of space.
Overexposure thins the scenes
Of our lives. It is a summer sun
In which we dream by the river,
Scheming for constancy, changing.

When the Night Falls

I crossed on the cables when it was late
To look at what I thought was a boat.
Earlier I'd seen the air illuminate
A white sycamore, thought even more
Marvelous the scene in my brain—
That the two were one. But not
For long. Still, given the path's aim,
The young will see it almost the same.
The painting will be similar, with different
Signature in the corner. Whenever I
Imagine being dead, I can't see
The world without an angle. My foot
Finds air instead of path, I stumble and
Lose my breath. I feel the phenomenology
Of self, no name of Applewhite, only bushes
And briars and undetermined shapes in the night—
Feel dissociate, and *far*. I'm almost out
Of the picture. The picture remains. Howl
From dog or owl comes scrambled and haunting.
The seat from a junked truck, one end
Sunk in ice near the bank, proves the boat
I'd thought. I find I've caught my leg
On the old barbed wire below the cable.
I hurry across hand over hand, almost
Take a tumble in the ice-crusted river.
The sycamore lighted by consciousness returns.
I'll run the sun while there is time.

In Sight of the Self

Current from rain last night
Crushes past, rapids with separate
Cordings like glistening muscle.
A lecture has made me late
But I feel at home in my house
Of clothes, poncho an envelope
Sealing heat. The dim chasm
Between banks of trees flows
With fog in the rain. I run
An inchoate terrain as in
Dreams, the soaked path slick
As shit, air half water, my
Breath only puff of fog and the
River a pavement of light
The mist diffuses. I ask
Myself what I am doing
Here in the night, if anyone
I know would recognize
The person they give my name.
I have left my poncho on
A limb and run on, too warm.
Now I return and find it
Like something hung by current,
Apart from me, yet shape of
A body. As the rain comes
Harder, I resume that part
Of myself, that house of breath.
Light grows late, shape of
The path approximate. I remember
A circular erasure
From seeing the sun. The rain
Spreads around its sound
In rings, as from the pebble
In a pond. I am the center
That drops out of sight:
Bullseye everything aims at,
Dot of the target.

Buzzard's Roost

As the ball world falls
Away downhill, only one point
Is flat: this moment.
Riding the quickly turning
Earth, I am spun into night.
Conception would run
In abstract strides,
Measuring distance
Like a draftsman's compass.
But below this geometer's
Diagram, the river is plowed
Into a harvest of flashes.
Its hot brilliance
Into peripheral vision
Stains with afterimage.
The current is my personal
Distance, the crooked going
That colors the straight light
With error. Crossing the cable,
I narrow my footing to one line.
On the farther side, I climb
The two-story house of stone,
Stand alone in a height
Of pure illumination. I see the Eno
Wrinkling and sliding
Fifty feet below, wearing
Reflection like sweat
On skin. The moment
Like a statue passes,
I kneel, dizzy, see
Moss in an ice-rimmed cup
Of rock. I walk the cable back,
Continue my narrow strand
Of time, composing
Its form
Line by line.

An Orphaned Voice

I came down to the swollen river.
Kingfisher stretched his straight flight
Away, white-collared, uniform priest
Of waters. I was left to the rapids'
Idiot merriment, fat splash and
Unconscious laughter. *Full. Full. I am*
Always young. Left alone to give
The torrent tongue, I was swept
Along in sympathy, no head in sight
Above the current's bucking bed:
Quilt of cream foam and sediment.
Whatever circles made by turtle or
Beaver had melted. Forms
Plunged back underwater. In that wet
Rattle, I listened hard for words
Of a father. Finally, from trees, came
The kingfisher's blue, electric chatter.

House of Seasons

Frost has browned these vines
That mound in the corner of vision, like
Forms from a dream. They don't determine
Decoration. October is buttoned by an
Aster's purple. Spring, so much closer,
Ignites in trout lilies' match flames,
Hepatica's blue porcelain. It is
In love, it is *being*. Jonquils
At the home site roofed only by evening
Greet me above the briared floor—
Sweet as, after long flight, the sight
Of my wife. By the river, I remember
How driving with my father
I'd imagine outside a giant figure
Stride-by-stride pacing the car. I run
Within that shadow, then return to the farm
Of only jonquils. A grown man, I bow
To the widows in yellow. As my nail
Snaps stems tense with sap,
I wonder who planted them—
Then walk with my wand of bloom
Home to the living woman I love.

The Water-Machine

What moves is the river's bottom layer.
It carries an aura, an envelope of continuing
Air, here where the path has disappeared in
The seamless grasses, the honeysuckle tangle.
Webs break on my face, as I still follow
This elastic animal, infinitely divisible,
Whose plastic mass knifed by snags rejoins
And rejoins, a divided whole always going.
I catch the sun over my shoulder. A molten
Hole gauges my moments, levels through
Vectors of limbs. I look from the round
Run of space to the crooked path. The word
Uterus comes sinuously to my mouth. I
Feel my brain an organic machine that
Yearns. Cell-sacs light up in eddies.
This binary flicker of matter,
Like the live river, can drift
And breathe. Can mean.

The Sex of Divinity

The blooms have mostly gone
But rains have come. The river runs
Bright tan. June is almost
Upon us. I feel weak at first on
The trail in this third week after
My respiratory virus. The foliage has
Massed so as to make one imagine
Some fossil forest compacted to a coal
Of green. Leaves screen the sun
So I can endure its hard shine,
Its bead-bright splintering rattle.
The far bank yields a wild astilbe.
I see the sun whole, a transparent orb.
This androgyne is round as mind,
To illumine within and without.
I break spider webs as I run.
High on Buzzard's Roost, I look down
As on my shirt the hundreds
Of strands my chest has collected
Stretch and glisten, shirt of Nessus
Or Lilliput cables I break as
I breathe, giant in thought.
My small circumference has caught
Fire from the fierce eye shining
Its sexual round through leaves.

Light Beyond Thought

I wonder what summer I remember? I
Sit in shadow, where a dust of pollen
On waterfloor moves with the broom of wind.
And gnats gyrate, lighter than dust,
Fluff on the wrist of the river,
Jumping to its pulse. Spider webs float,
Dragonflies chase each other, and the sycamore
Leaning over from the opposite shore,
Its trunk in splotches like quarters,
Like camouflage, is almost silver. Its
Roots exposed by erosion flow
And mold like concrete, a scaffolding
Intricate as water in limestone—
Like the roots of memory. Mountain
Laurel blazes in flower. Green seems
To create its own meaning. This long
Day's sun, still high, seems frozen.
Glistens too richly to question.

Out of My Circle

Vines coil, dull in their greenness—
Three-leaved, poisonous. Turtles
In the ponds of bends
Slide under. A snake's shed
Skin and first blackberries
Mark beginning of summer.
Hepatica, foam flower,
No longer sign their names
With wands of bloom. The ego,
Not to grow ill, must
Go out of its circle. Dead
Water shrinks in the shape
Of a target, black-wet
Silt around it. Whatever
Life it surrounds now names
Itself with splash or wriggle.
In order not to grow ill,
I must travel. All biology
Stirs here in this womb of mud
But is not self-aware.
I must see my life from afar.
As I am driving westward,
Land through the windshield
Will hit a center it aims at:
Self that pivots horizons about
Its point. In sun on rocks
In the stream, I seem to feel
The wind of driving. Snake slips,
Half-seen, from the rock
Below my feet, pours his black
Length back into the river
Like a bitter drink. Not
To grow ill, we must learn to speak.

Prayer for My Son

The low river flows like smoked glass.
Small bass guard their nest. Next
To our house, the cardinals in their
Crabapple feed two open mouths.
Parents and offspring, we flex
And swing in this future's coming,
Mirror we look into only darkly.
My youngest is boarding an airplane
To a New York he's never seen.
Raised in such slumberous innocence
Of Bible schools and lemonade,
I adjust poorly to this thirst for
Fame, this electronic buzz prizing
Brilliance and murderers. Oh son,
Know that the psyche has its own
Fame, whether known or not, that
Soul can flame like feathers of a bird.
Grow into your own plumage, brightly,
So that any tree is a marvelous city.
I wave from here by this Indian Eno,
Whose lonely name I make known.

The Bison

In the Tetons, hiking up Paintbrush canyon,
I lifted up more than my weight along
That trail, its soil filled with round stones
From glaciers. Mount Woodring was immediately
Above to my right, through the lodgepole pines.
There above seven thousand feet, air tasted
Thin on the tongue. Vistas of Wyoming
Sagebrush, a dirt road that cut from the highway,
To run thirty miles toward the horizon,
Had drawn my emptiness. A squirrel had narrowly
Escaped, where a pavement matted with bloody fur
Showed the jackrabbits' ignorance of shortest distances.

Beyond a cleft of shade, I saw a hawk arc out
Suddenly from cliff's gloom, wing feathers
Translucent in that wall of illumination.
The great pane that held my walk shifted
Steadily nightward, like a mountain-tall
Transparent glacier whose yellow tone deepened.
In the canyon beyond the pines, Jenny Lake
Was aluminum in the moose grass of Jackson Hole.
Clouds seemed to scrape the stone spires,
To attach for a moment, flags of breath-fog.
The monkshood was waist high, Indian paintbrush
Flaming in patches, and, higher, in wet ledges
By the cascade, villages of white columbine.
A backpacker returning said it was too late now
For Holly Lake. I went on faster, dry breath
Quick and the pulse beating lightly in my ears.
A French family passing through the cut
Above the falls said Holly Lake was not so far.
The teen-agers were long-legged, hairless, light
On the rocks as antelope. In the fern around
The next bend, the pink succulent flowers
Camped by the rapids turned all my breath
To bright color. I remembered the Continental Divide,
That bleak horizon beside the Interstate,

The Peterbilt diesels blasting up the one slope,
Coasting down the other. No higher trail in view.
But here, the glaciers on the Teton walls
Let down their streamers of water, white
Feathers blowing in that late afternoon
Of all time. I inhaled that flame of wind,
Knew the Durham I would go back to,
The imperfect setting for my imperfect self,
Would be enough. Would be all that I could
Reach this afternoon, remembering the mist
At Colter Bay, above glacial Jackson Lake,
Whose water-ground stones of red and gray
And slate green were lined across their pitted
Smoothness with a layering beginning in
The Cretaceous sea. I made it as far as
Holly Lake, came down in the sunset and
Its afterglow to String Creek, where a mule deer,
Drinking, bounded away some paces, eyeing me
With black nose and tall ears focused,
Allowing me its world. In almost-night
On the road back toward the campground, the silhouette
Crossing the light had shoulders thicker than any moose.
The matted, godly brow, the eyes only implied
Below those headdress horns, configured an urge:
A shadow still alive with wildflowers, the craggy wind.

Bridge Back Toward the South

Saturday night, driving toward the Mississippi bridge
On Missouri highway fifty-one, drinking beer,
Listening to the country radio, four thousand
One hundred and forty-four miles
Newly on the odometer, I stop at a tavern
To ask my way across. The barmaid stretches
Her jeans with easy flesh and ignorance.
The one table of customers are all drunk.
A kid drinking Dr Pepper alone at the bar
Explains how I should go. When I come
Into the diffused glow of lights from
The river not yet seen, that expands from
Below the road-level—like an air I could drive on—
I can almost forgive the South
For this ball of feeling in my throat.

Driving Toward Cairo

I've lost the route leading
Here. I know only this
Deep river, these barns and cornfields
And a telephone line—two wires
Between the spaced poles—to remind
Me of our connection and of our
Loneliness. And the church
Past the village of Anna, past
Jonesboro, where Lincoln debated,
Square small steeple transmitting
The sweet sad assurance of those
Hymns. The apple tree with
Green fruit, the crepe myrtle
Blazing, the double silos
As the sun comes out. This
Illinois landscape holds
A home I've never known.

Rivers

Campsites in Nebraska, Wyoming, Tennessee
Will never take the print of my shoulders
Again. Five-thousand-odd miles have
Wound into memory. I find it has rained.
Today, the gray silt in the Eno shows me
The body of the muddy Illinois.
When clouds pile reflections
On its face, it will imitate
The mighty Ohio. Clear, green,
It will be the Snake in Wyoming.
Oh Vermillion, Spoon, Meramec,
Tennessee, Caney Fork, Shoshone,
Missouri, Kanawha, Little Blue,
Cedar, Platte, Medicine Bow.
As the Eno runs in its same
Way, it catalogues your names.

The Self, that Dark Star

There in the Tetons at nine thousand feet,
The Eno thinned on my tongue.
Now that I am home, it is thinned
By autumn. As I walk the trail back,
Those time zones I've driven
Hover above my shoulders.
As I am spun to the East,
I taste their singing. No matter
How I run, a vacant land
Westward observes the last sun.
It may be that such land is my own:
Cheyenne, salted with hail, under
Bolts like the end.
The center of me empties, a cyclone's.
Like eyes which have stared at horizons.
I found desert and flood,
No ego-restoration. Perhaps
This hole in identity, this loss
Of self which is poetry,
This being like a collapsed sun hoarding
Its rays—is the *I* of me. If I am
A yearning, simply, a gravity—
If, star fathers who
Have erased me, I have no
Brighter surface—may these
Mountains and rivers, one bison, shine
Their denser radiation
As they vortex into your son.

Sleeping with Stars and Bulbs, Time and Its Signs

Now the year is gone, I lie proleptically
Down in the same winter in which I
Began to run. Trees taller than this pillow
Of earth their leaves feather is round
Stand above. Dreams falter near the fallen
Chimney stones, vines binding them to my
Forehead and to a cedar. In my tent that blocks
Orion, I listen with one ear against earth
For each jonquil bulb alive in the abandoned homestead.
The spading fork I hid in weeds two seasons ago
Is rusting quietly, in the same time-order as these
Relics of the astral family, whose rafters are outlined
By branches overhead. A hinge in subsoil swings their door
Upon a room full of space. China pieces cohere
Like stars in the Coalsack nebula. Each jonquil bulb
Sacked here begins to unsheathe its single green claw
Which will dig a yellow from night.
Flowers through my memory of their numbers
Gather the slope below us into one expanse,
Where the names of brothers, cut in bark in 1911,
Near the Model-T carcass, unearth the artifacts
Of Henry Ford's century—recovering the pitted
Drive shaft, from farm rows that the trees have
Again underfoot. I feel myself half-invisible: as thin
Against air as these brothers, with their father and mother.
Taken back over by nature's left-handedness,
I turn over, heavily, in my bag. The arbitrary
Connectives of language, composted below me
With crockery and jawbone, stem in time
As between the bulb and its flower. Those transplanted
To my own house will ring times in and out when
It also is a branch-sketched cinder of rafters.
Tonight, still, I expand in drowsiness—
Feel my huge shadow gravity-held,
On the physical basis of all poetry,
Nailed to earth's wheel by the stars.

VII

The War Against Nature

On the roof of my father's station
During World War Two, a one-room tower
Was built all windows, with phone
And identification manual. Quicker
Than any of the men, I'd see the plane
And know its type, call out its name.

Heat ponded that wet atmosphere,
Where tobacco stirred like kelp. Our only
Hope was spotting silhouette in far air.
Why out of the blazing surfaces do we
Desire these forms, these lines sharp-edged
As thought can whet? What privileged

Paradigm lives in first dream,
In the hands' planing of a balsa arrow,
To float on some humid, afternoon stream
Made by wind, as the thunderheads grow?
Bored with a primordial green,
We wanted experimental designs we'd seen,

The fire it'd have meant had an enemy
Plane appeared. Men returned to the farm,
Volunteers fell away. I watched a bare sky,
Memorizing the chart of possible form:
Messerschmitt, Wellington, workhorse Douglas.
Ideas absolute as the blue emptiness.

The Student Pilot Sleeps

The propeller is feathered, allows
Us to soar. The silence seems hours.
What shadows my view through the window,
Below, is the gray battle dun
Of Werner Mölders' Bf-109.

As he rises in place beside us,
His face in the square-paned greenhouse
Contorts with grief. His hands press the glass.
He is flying a Gustav, with bulbous spinner,
Grease and field repairs of the last winter

Of the war. Then Johnnie Johnson
Is beside him in his long-nosed Spitfire
IX, elliptical wings with prongs of cannon.
Suddenly I see fast-climbing Sailor Malan
In his Mark I flown in the Battle of Britain.

Soon I am leading a *schwarme*, then a circus
Including four-engined Gothas with the radiators
Of trucks, their biplane wings like suspension
Bridges. Max Immelmann makes his famous
Turn and the Red Baron displays aviators

He has killed with silhouettes on his scarlet
Albatross. All planes ever lost, all pilots,
Gather behind my wings. Roger my fatherly
Instructor is oblivious to the terrible formation
I trail in air from my haunted imagination.

Lessons in Soaring

for Roger Hivert, and the GROB

Sky looks cloudy. It will lighten,
You say. You give me instructions—
Hard to understand in your French accent—
Degrees of bank through the unfamiliar headset,
Extents of the imperfect circles of turns.
I must watch the amorphous horizon,

Which fades into rain through the canopy,
Spins sidewise about our tightening spiral.
I pull on the stick, keep our flight level.
In the green-blur below, you teach me to see
The numbered highway, our straight runway.
I practice the patterned descent, to free

Myself of you, to come back someday solo.
You make me see, through mists swirled
Muddily, the correct heading, the land's form,
The city on the horizon—to guess its name.
Not ready to be without you in this world
We must shape, I hesitate as we slow

Before the stall. Have you taught me all
You are permitted? Why can I not see
The landmarks more easily, why is the plastic
Bubble scratched and dirtied? I need clarity
Of vision instantly over the map, an automatic
Adjustment of wing to wind, a gull's soul.

I need all you've never told me, Roger.
I can't face these misted cities alone,
This powerline-towered, forested terrain.
Below these controlling movements, flying
Still evades my search for its meaning.
May I gather from your years aloft the father

I need? Just as we curve into the pattern
To land, I notice colors of trees, how green
Looks new from down low, how the quarry
Glints its granite, rows of fields are orderly.
The one beside me is my wiser double,
Who changes our plane into a single crystal.

Then in a moment we have landed.
I lose perspective in the checklist detail,
In wheeling our bird toward the hangar, plans
For tomorrow, unwritten poems, pain of the ended
Ascent. I've lost my soaring self again—
Alone with the GROB, fiberglass nightingale.

Art and the Garden

for Jonathan Lasker, Manhattan

Figured against a feminine ground,
Woman became thought's paradigm.
His blunt thrust to understand
Exceeded the garden, inventing time.
He rose inside her vase of skin,
Plucked by flowers to central Eden.

He wanted surfaces white as Eve's
But made by man, with gate and tower.
He wanted the garden to conceive.
"But green if burned by mind deflowers
Itself" the angel argued. "Your own eyes,
Possessing fruits and hers, are fires."

Another quoted the words of Mammon.
He knew the luxury of objects, the quest
Of pitiless will to know, driving on
In pleasure, until one's own likeness burst
From womb-earth, founding in perpetuity
The measured marble spires of a city.

The painter left her smoothness framed
In gold. They crowded close, to see her
Borne on scallop shell, see each famed
Rape by swan or bull. The perceiver
Kept his clothes on—she on the grass
Violated in her absolute nakedness.

Museums hold her glory, their walls
The color of cinders, where Olympia's stare
Reflects our own stale eyes, our falls.
The bare, forked thing lay unaware;
Mind learned art and to possess,
Possessing itself in consciousness.

The Failure of Southern Representation

for Jonathan Silver, sculptor

I

Sunlight's impasto on brightleaf has not yet
Curled wet-lipped, no moccasin-caduceus on cypress has
Slithered in succulent gesture. Unrepresentable
Vacancies blotch the historical record, as invisibly
The dead bitch bares teeth in the mud ditch.
Within the undetermined census of these pines,
Beside these sobbings, lynchings, cries extracted like
Turpentine from resin, no palette has tar enough.
Under even this present burn of noon no cadmium
Or zinc is vivid as the life, the art is choked.
Expressways paved over the past cannot express,
Though sheet metal signs rise yellow as tobacco,
Are veined by collisions and hurricanes. Shopping centers
With their tourist pastels are dumb as tombs in this land
Still furious with its phantoms. This surface can be neither
Painted nor spoken, no oxymoronic pigment is mixed
To render livid noon as coal midnight. Footsoldiers'
Shove and charge imitated by commercial assault
Cannot cohere into this silence of vista
Still as the coral shelf under green fathoms.

II

Memorial heads outside the libraries erode
And disassemble, tar-dark patches like spots of shame
Inhabiting the marble. Names implanted in this terrain —
Civil War heroes, progenitors of civic virtue — fall ill
As I look. Limestone flakes blow away in wind
Like flesh dropping in leprosy. Yet this also is
Inaccurate, hypothetical. The columned, white plantation
Invents itself on front porches now wholly vanished,
Inherited from fictitious aunts, fabulous uncles.
Accents which deep in their vowels have
Never given up the slaves come back
To haunt us, a chorus, a convention of narration.

III

Music. Music more probably represents, if we admit
That the fall of moonlight on tidal rivers cannot
Be heard or suggested, that negro spirituals,
Condensed into an atmosphere of pain,
Erode the stelae in Confederate cemeteries
To namelessness, to silence. That now we number
The thud of boxes from eighteen-wheelers
At docks in Atlanta, the diesel thug thug,
The tin clang of dimes buying polyester scarves,
As glass tones from stereos strike tin
Horizons, where barns are pinned to burn
In the unvoiced uproar of glare.

A Place and a Voice

I

A veteran hickory on the ridge
against a sky turned gun metal
blue by the fall of snow

merged with my thought of you:
voice impervious to surgery
though the trunk, lopped, incised,

is not what I remember.
Yet the body still supports
breath, that line of words

unreeling out of a head.
Region and history. Fate,
if one wants to call it that.

II

Saul Erastus Mercer.
Minister and father. Mother
Ethel Waldo, learned woman,

author for the magazine
of shut-ins. Herself wheelchaired
with damaged knee, rheumatic

heart. Was her fall down
stairs the same as your father's?
Or wasn't he thrown under

the wheels of his buggy? Did
he recover? Or live with wheel
marks on his belly, as I'd

imagine? The porcelain white
cat—why did it powder your
navy frock with hairs, on the car

ride to Richmond? What was
the sequence of places? Weldon,
Maxton, Raleigh, Burlington,

Durham? Could you call
no place your home? Must
a Methodist, if superintending

a district, bleed his family's
health for a godlier flock?
The white behind your brow

I hear today was always there
in your face, even before age:
White of the wooden parsonages.

III

So you settled the problem
of dislocation with father
and Stantonsburg: the wrestler

come home again to his footing
in this thousand-person town
like a stump in a swamp.

You endured the house on one side
of the street near his parents—
his favored sister settled

on the other. Your revenge was sons.
Virginia had only a daughter.
We were your own, but men.

IV

You allowed our world
paper pens crayons knives
trains clay balsa bombs:

fused or thrown, grenades
in blue clouds into the street,
as we fought our war against quiet.

Dad's motors hummed and roared.
I sang behind the mower, powered
over weeds and briars in vacant

lots. Our religion forbad not
noise, or toys, or firecrackers,
including Vesuvius fountains—

their mountains of sparks in darkness
almost as good as limb-pyre after
the old oak fell. We stirred and

watched the showers of gold
ascending into the stars. Starved
minds never lived in our house.

Was it really the South? Life was
rich, authentic. Sunlight in air seemed
a wheat we breathed as we worked.

We plowed the sand pit pond with
a scarlet boat. The doctor's blond
wife flashed her breasts as

a wave washed over the towed
innertube—stretched slit of rubber—
where she sat. Not to murder

desires in their cradle, I sowed
my seed in the field, later yielded
to the Ferris wheel sensation

in my car topped off with gas from
our Esso station, pockets rich
with condoms in foil coins.

First love, you were sunlight,
starlight, utterly intoxicant
to hold, were mountains and

valley under the air in the flat
fields there in the bug-winged night—
lightning bugs sparking the windows.

V

So, mother, I knew everything
except for you. My heart breaking,
I'd lain nights in prayer, asking

that you not die. Beyond the door,
something that shook it with silent uproar
threatened your life. I could not hear.

I could not know of the stunning pressure
bottled by your body, between the pure
legacy of your father and what you had to endure

from your husband's family: slights
to you as outsider, Sunday nights
when he'd abandon you for the rites

of a good son come home, obediently
listening to William Henry's piety—
at the piano, "Sunrise tomorrow for me."

Women at the time could only feel.
You could not interfere in the real
world of his war-work he'd reveal

in flashes at supper, as the storm
hovered the town and increased an alarm
you felt perpetually, inflicting all harm

you feared or wished on yourself alone.
Tension increased in the house. Stone
could not have born anxiety of one

son with rheumatic heart, the other
with infected ear and scarlet fever—
the doctors uncertain, prescribing in error.

Your nerves were bad, necessarily.
And yet we led a life, were happy
in our way. Air was alive with the play

of lightning. After the war, a roar
from motors of greater horsepower
intensified plans. You'd always hear.

We utilized you as our atmosphere.
For my football drama, you were theater.
For the thread of my story, listener.

VI

Later I resented the emotional claim.
How could I be a man on my own
and confess to you as prodigal son?

If an inner compass turned toward
home, how could I find a reward
in the North of studies? No coward,

I fought on fields not of my choosing,
in Gettysburgs of examinations, searing
nights of physics, logic, drunken partying.

The final thing I resented was not
that expectation of listener like one's own thought,
but the magnetic resonance your part

of the earth had, and the outcast half-
life I felt when away by myself—
even later, with my own wife.

I hated that you and a place were one,
so vivid a myth, claustrophobic Eden,
rich Atlantis in which to drown.

Most of my life I've been a settler,
clearing an emotional heart-room larger
by the year, being, to less land, a stranger.

Now that I am here and you are there,
we talk on Sundays over a wire.
I listen to your childhood, admire

your ride in Durham on a white horse
toward a stable for a friend, to a house
they were tearing down. Your father fell of course

because constantly you were moving,
parsonages roomier and colder, spring
only a dream and the cat's fur snowing.

Memory wanders from Robeson County
to Raleigh to your father. I follow to each city,
feeling knowledge grow with each address, sea

to mountain. If your voice traveled far enough,
I might inhabit the earth.

Greenhouse Effect

Abandoned pavement beside the overpass
Led left, into the weeds' dead end.
Sequencings of pink and yellow pastel
Perfected the leaves behind a kind of glass.
Foliage looked ripened, used, as though the wood
Were a body after knowledge, its deep blood
Suffused against the surface as from love, or bruise.
The fur-rag beside the road signaled *dead animal.*
Mixed weeds in fields with sourwood floods
Wavered maroon as Brahms. A little fever
Touched the air. The mater once was fecund-willful,
Her maggot-tendrils twisted in the loam's dark sleep.
Now her autumn flush seemed hectic, ill.
The profundity of sky beyond cerise was never
More a music. Seeing her sick, I felt a lyric escape
Lift from the mundane, like a jetliner's transcendent
Rush. The abandoned asphalt when I walked it
Was hushed by pine brush, except for the silk whish
Of cars. A tunnel toward the future made an arch:
Overgrown, and stained by a scrim of exhaust—as if green
Had marked a season without meaning.

The Descent

You must drive to these little towns
(Appie, or Seven Springs)
Expecting nothing.
You must find in the general store
More than you came for;
These olives in glass, deviled ham in tins,
These letters of labels
As from the box of eight crayons—
Colors of the new alphabet
That once outlined first figure
On canvas empty as a mirror.
Then, you couldn't imagine yet
How light would be bent, and wet.
How birdsong would be muted
And your innocence learn the sordid
Involvement with its new vesture:
Each fold and slit of the creature.
So this was the descent of the soul
You say, buying a ginger ale.
This is as it was when you were young.
This was the shelved house
Holding all experience for the mouth.
The Japanese paper umbrellas were next door.
White lattice upon the second floor
Made your prison bars, a porch
Like a first grade stool
Where your bird soul could perch
And practice its song of flutter
And fall, thrusting its tongue
Into darknesses like molasses.
Oh these towns, these elementary classes.
You pause on the sheltered walk,
For a moment in the pane
Of that earlier world, when all
Was excruciating, pristine.
The car you drive is a kind of burial.
You promise yourself to come again.

A Conversation

I

Our connection still uncertain as prayer,
I hear you at the other end of the wire
Adjusting the aid to your better ear.
Why you in your country only ninety miles away
Should sound transatlantic, is not explained.
A pseudo-yankee who has left the home land,
I scarcely deserve a reply.
Yet we both assume an inheritance,
Our discussion of the crop a pledge of allegiance.

II

I saw your figure as in the distance:
Forcing the evening mower through the resistance
Of grasses and darkness, piloting your boat
Across fields the flood had claimed, Contentnea
Creek in its loop toward Ruffin's Bridge a Tiamat
Twisting loose from her bounds.
Intent over the wheel, like one who founds
An empire or a city, you plowed a sea
Of sky not separate from water and the earth.
There might have been a black bull and a white
Pulling your prow like a copper blade
Around a perimeter the mortal gods had made.
You would have finished the lawn by night,
Lightning bugs like the stars in their instants of birth.

III

Later at the station you commanded,
The leader who committed his outnumbered
Troops to combat. The greasepit would rattle
With machine gun exhaust from a pipe overhead.
As I fired into fittings, my brothers in battle
Were Ralph ex-Marine, country-music James, Bill who read
Detective novels at least: veterans who told
Me how to survive, lie low, hose mud

From three counties from underneath fenders, pick gold
Coin prophylactic wrappers without comment
From the cracks of back seats. They saw my blood
Pressing high in my chest, like the summit
Of a thundercloud. They knew what your rules allowed
And how to evade. They joked of the world
When darkness came, and I could claim what girl
I chose and ride the carnival Ferris wheel
In fact or in metaphor. But what war
Made it necessary that I prefer,
To your hard truth, their lenient error?

IV

Now that my hearing goes a little,
I listen to you better, that old crackle
Of static on the line a re-run of afternoons
When the radio's news caught storms like distant guns.
I have your mouth from the Rock Ridge Barneses,
The Applewhite upper back. With Ralph you lifted the block
Of a motor, crushed a disc. Before your sons,
Your buckled on the supporting corset like an armor.
You never allowed us to see you fail.
Prayer for you was never a metaphor,
And with will like a blade you cut trail
Through our thicket of misadventure. The wreck
I got into with your car when drunk
Was forgiven without lost temper. The only lecture
Came on your boat aground in the empty garage.
I held no grudge, but continued the miscarriage
Of your justice. No son can accept a pure
Commandment as in stone. Yet I desired
The flame of your will, your single word.

V

The conversation comes to an end.
Imagination stretched along a wire can extend

No farther. How can I understand the belief
That has supported you over the hot coals of grief
These years? In the post-operative support hose
Your legs showed muscle like the wrestler you were,
Or dancer. You walked on fire, would close
Your jaws as if wired, refuse the drug.
You quick-stepped later through the ruptured gall bladder,
Amazed the surgeon with your steel. I hug
You now, on visits, realize as I press
Your work-forged shoulders how some mightiness
Descends to sons, mysterious to the both of us.

VI

The unconscious still sees your face glowing like iron.
For the inalterable child of sleep, you are earth born,
One of the Titans. Your deafness is not physical,
Though I share it. A distance not overcome
Pedestals your demands on yourself and your sons
Like a statue. Condemned to be dumb
And suppliant before power we must also embody,
We live reserved from our anger, fearful lest we destroy.
A veteran, I salute the lost commander,
Pledge false allegiance to the flag of tobacco.
I see you now on visits as the aging
Father I love, find you now even tender
In your affections, in your devotion to mother.
And I worship and regret the other figure,
The god-king I once wished dead,
The scriptural presence whose lips read
Me commandments under mountainous cloud,
Moses-chiseled by His voice aloud.

VII

On the day when finally you will have died,
How will I imagine the flood-wide
Grasses in Wilson, Pitt, or Greene County,

Without you as mechanic of each mower—
You, who made my first covenant with that sea
As I followed your effort behind the leveling reel
While it spun cut blades into dusk? Abraham, Noah,
Your wake upon our lawn was like a boat's
And always I will see you as you float
The untamed creek, overpassing fences at the wheel,
Your motor in that silence the Word of a reflected sky.
How can I feel but elegy
For the figure of language you've left with me?
Help me father, I say as in prayer, to hear
A son's new testament, fairer writ. As the wire's
Voice, heard last, crackles with the old fire.

VIII

Storm in the Briar Patch

In obedience and ignorance, okra
      stalks, gaunt as prisoners, stand
where screens only keep the flies in.
      Dry season and the boy's father
slaps him for no reason it seems—
      rutted landscape fallen to ruin,
pokeweed veined like a hand
      where the scraps of laundry hang,
flap like the wrung-necked rag of
      a chicken in its arcs. Storm
seems a long time coming and strong
      when it dooms down. Spark
crack connects the sky and land
      with copper-green scar in the eye,
as the cat trembles, the three fish
      wait to be cleaned. The lean-tos
lean into the wind, lean as bean-
      poles, the beans dangling, jangled
like wind chimes, while farmers damn
      the hail as it holes tobacco: broad
as banana leaves, like small roofs but
      pierced now, a punctured infantry.
After, he goes the rounds of his fields, each
      hill shredded, a mimic-man, a sham of
what life might be—ghost of a crop to go
      up from a match in cloud and
gesture, not shiver here, broken, long
      hours of raising ruined in his eyes.

Home Team

There was a stillness about the games, afternoons,
      something to be decided, but in suspension—a runner
taking his lead as the pitcher eyed him suspiciously,
      the outfielders glancing back at the bushes thirty
feet to their rear, edging in a little, trying to remember
      the soft spots, where a line drive wouldn't bounce up.
Thunderheads building in the sky enveloped the scene within
      an elemental light. The thickening, varnishlike quality
of water in air, and heat—the pure clarity beginning to
      congeal—would capture this space at the edge of a village,
gathering the figures into one impression, while a fly ball
      hit long toward right center hung up against the base
of a cloud, the crowd rising to its feet as the runner on first
      broke joyously for second, toward home. Charlie Boykin,
coming around the bases, grinned with the mouths of small boys
      under the tree, their biceps thicker as they looked at his.
So the game and those summers continued. But Charlie Justice
      played for the Redskins, his figure ghostly in the electronic
snow of T.V.—not on a field near the one that Willie
      Mozingo had plowed, before he took his chunky body into
far left field, a two-legged gleam in his cream-colored uniform,
      as afternoon deepened and the slanting sun made balls hard
to judge but he caught them anyway, back in the broom sedge.
      Fred Pittman signed the minor-league contract and people
went to Wilson to see him. The diamond was left to high-
      school games, to frog creak and owl whoop in midsummer
evenings, and the lightning bugs coming on in a space that
      held the stars. Houses in sight of the diamond oak
lit up their windows with the glow of T.V. Always a few
      farm boys, not risking injury, hit rocks toward the trees
with broomsticks, or prevailed on a younger brother to throw
      them one more pitch down the middle, so they could drive
the baseball over the weeded ditch, out of the pasture.

A Wilson County Farmer

The mercury-vapor yard light on a pole
      comes on automatically at dusk, triggered
it seems by the television's phosphorescent glow in
      the front room, seen incongruously through those
sashes and panes from just after the Civil War.
      The middle-aged farmer standing in shadow of this
unnatural light before his packhouse, still smoking
      a Lucky, just a few in any day now, sees
heads of his wife and daughter-in-law through the
      window, and the grandson's occasional, ball-quick
passage through color, and thinks maybe he has survived
      too long. Life is easier, maybe, with MH-30
to inhibit suckers, the tractor-drawn harvesters,
      where croppers ride close to the ground, breaking
off leaves, clipping them into the reeled chains. But hands
      are undependable, and without his blood kin,
a man couldn't hardly be sure of a harvest crew.
      Some use the migrants, hard-working, ignorant
of the ways of tobacco. With the quotas, the declining
      prices, every day more news about cancer, this man
who learned tobacco from his father, who himself couldn't
      read and write, looks far across at red Antares
over the swamp woods there beyond the highway, not knowing
      what star he is seeing, and feels his station in this
place lit by blue light and T.V. as odd and as lonely.

Time at Seven Springs: An Elegy

Aware of the house suspended in a riverward slippage,
      he inhabits a self invented in language, who once existed.
The boy and his grandfather approach a white, disused hotel.
      They see the Neuse, sullen in heat, icicles of Spanish moss
inverted on its surface. As Maxwell wrestles his grandfather's demijohn,
      the boy confounds their stories; remembers other conversations.
A moment lost to his consciousness rises with the voices and waters.
      In an outhouse over the river, he returns his trickle to the current.
He is one with the families who had stayed the week for treatment,
      filling the hotel. We take part in his liquid wishing, search
for the selves we were, and are; overhear as he recalls his father,
      too Methodist for the fisherman's muddy worship but aware of
Contentnea in bridge-air, an animal all tail, that might be ridden.
      Their speedboat's moment of capsize revolves in slow motion,
to bring him night: under the hull like a swallowed Jonah. He is rescued
      to consciousness, finds himself later in his grandfather's study,
wishing the awareness of Seven Springs water. In shadow, he drinks.
      Gum leaves floated red and red-green, only star-points touching
at first on the underground-seeming drainage, silt slipping like
      poured coffee or molasses, suspended in moving but always moving,
imperceptibly as the line of barn-shadow advancing in the farmyard
      as work went on and never was there time enough to finish.
A vision went out from him, knowing by imagining the land he was
      now apart from. A shadow-edge detached from the eaves and
slid over cropland and orchard, elongating shade beyond the rib-
      sided farmhouses, dividing tin roofs exactly along ridgelines.
Oak leaves clung tightly to the ground as a pressure of light
      swept mule lots and yards with tractors, laying down
figures lengthened by their passing. Heavy-armed women looped on
      the last of the tobacco. His grandfather's father, wounded
in the Civil War, disintegrated further in the graveyard across
      from the homeplace, while Toisnot Swamp a half mile away
sucked at his bones, thirsty for their decay. He feels his loss
      while it makes so complete a picture — not that the vision is untrue
but that his seeing it marks it as over. A wind blows hard over
      field rows, dusting their tops with a sugary mica, swinging

arms of cornstalks. Sweet gum balls let go their prickly hold on
      clay and flee like turned-up field mice, bumping onto pavement.
A train whistle dwindles into distances, trailing the metal vacuum
      of machines in passing, their whir and suction, as a mill-sound
busies the air, and mechanical harvesters first chug their awkward
      way along ditches and crop rows. The praying-mantis combines
stoop to cotton with a reverent humming, blowing lint into bins.
      His high-school classmates face toward him, framed in albums,
fading in good-bye, kids grown lean from side meat and collards,
      who went into the army, getting a little fatter, then departing
for jobs in cities, only grandmothers left, to be visited at Christmas,
      in the houses where the grandchildren's hearts still lingered.
He says farewell on paper, believing that for a region to be so
      changed it must also complete itself, that the sorrow of tobacco
will no longer haunt the soil, except from pits for marl
      and from burial knolls. The barns' fierce marks on horizons,
when fiery with curing, become the gesture that defined one era,
      an error necessary to discover, that his people in their history
had been driven to dress their aspirations in — those gaunt barns
      leaning as if to be taller against the twilight, as family
Bibles are muddied by a flood that consigns their names to the past.

After *Winslow Homer's Images of Blacks*

A Visit from the Old Mistress crystallizes into a single moment
the staggering realization faced by all Southerners after the Civil
War—both black and white—that things will never again be the
same.—Peter H. Wood and Karen C. Dalton, *Winslow Homer's
Images of Blacks: The Civil War and Reconstruction Years*

One born where the vines coil richly, where
      honeysuckle infatuates the air, feels
memory as reflex—to be fended off, succumbed to.
      The man who is running in a Piedmont
forest has kept himself slender because those
      he was born with have bellies that stretch
their shirts. He senses a movement behind him,
      the Forest Service pickup trailing its dense
cloud in August. He steps aside to let it pass,
      covering his nose with his shirt. The dust
boils up like the steam from a locomotive—
      coming at him in a fog bank: gray, elemental,
enclosing him in a different season. A drizzle
      weighs the air, so that these cabins that don't
rise high seem taller. The doors that frame
      the figures are set in rain as in a wall.
Their lips have his name on them, and one of these,
      a matron with a chest like a rubbery valley,
brown Bit, was his mother for a time. Their head-
      cloths are blue or red, the joints of the old
ones swollen. Now they are moaning softly, it is
      the pain-song of everyday work, of hidden
selves, of roles worn habitually, to please even him,
      when he was young. His own parents stand between
the cabins, diminished in stature, as if two dolls.
      They are saying with their eyes and lips that it
was hurt and humiliation they inherited, and allowed
      him to share in—a poor fare like collards boiled
until vitamins were gone, like corn bread with flavoring
      of ashes, beans and fatback, bits of language,

in the iron pot over the open fire, in the cabin
　　　where the woman in her apron is stirring it,
moving the long spoon, not speaking. "Bit," he calls,
　　　but she has forgotten him. His memory of her
is inadvertent, resilient as beds of pine needles—
　　　is a smell of side meat, colored by a quilt.
The dust has gathered thickly and receded. The thin
　　　film left on the dogwood leaves beside him seems
a legacy which has grayed his hair and eyebrows,
　　　showing him at middle age for a moment like
one of the elders: those on porches who remembered.

　　　He continues the path before him. Through a grove,
the tire trails are that elementary farmyard
　　　sand, silica the rain has eroded, and beside,
brown of loblolly needles: irreducible colors
　　　from his past, the pale and the brown together,
not mixing. A dove calls, bitter with pine scent.

The Cemetery Next to Contentnea

Births and deaths were at home. Farm wives bore
        children in double beds, whose mattresses remembered
their conceptions—birth stains and death stains never
        entirely washed from pads and quilts. And though farm-
hardy, one or more of the ten or twelve would not survive—
        what with flu, scarlet fever, whooping cough, mumps,
infections when all the doctor would do was puncture
        the eardrum. With his black snap bag in his buggy,
the doctor was little more help than the preacher. Midwives
        delivered babies, neighbor women who knew how to tie
off the cord and cut it, who had talked the mother through
        the worst pain, and now handed her the red little
face just squeezed out like a pea between fingers.
        People lived and died as their destiny let them;
home remedies placated rashes with boiled peach
        leaves or a dusting of cornmeal, and fat meat
with a drop of turpentine would draw out the splinter.
        The close-fitting belly band held in the infant's navel,
and purgations with castor oil seemed a punishment
        and forgiveness of the body. Life was statistical,
for those left after the night-agony, when a wind seemed
        rushing through the house, the oil lamps flickering
at the end. All linens would be boiled and the room
        opened up to the air, the floor and the walls scrubbed.
The raw earth in a graveplot on a rise across the road
        showed a mound that would settle over years. Gradually
medicine grew helpful, with ether for setting broken bones,
        vaccinations for smallpox, diphtheria, typhoid fever.
Survivable operations began to be performed in hospitals
        in small cities: Wilson, Goldsboro, New Bern, places
of last resort, where the grief-stricken couple might take
        their screaming child in their new automobile late
at night: museumlike corridors smelling of disinfectant.
        People who had faced birth and death straight on took
parents and children to these houses of collective mourning,
        and let the white screens, the gauzes, bandage away sight

of the vagina that gaped after birth, blood trickling out of it;
    of the convulsive throes and gasps of final breaths.
But farm folk continued to surround the dying, like
    the birth giving, with a family presence, waiting in
couples and cross-generational groupings in public lobbies,
    standing in the corridor outside the door at the end,
coming in for a last hoarse word, a hand-squeeze, a kiss
    with dry lips. And the funerals in white wooden churches
with graveside services kept on, even if the buried
    were no longer in plots in the fields, stones squared away
from the corn by fences—wrought iron softened by rust,
    no longer as hard as the blackberry bramble around it.

A Father and Son

They have put in their canoe at Grifton.
          It may be any year but is a present, because
the man was once a son upon such water, and now is
          father. For a time, creek kinks like a snake.
Deerflies bite where they sweat. From the letting
          go of shore, they have moved in a different sequence.
Oaks and hickories become poplars and ironwoods, always
          as end to the vista—the high banks casting image
on the water, the still trees magnificent, polished,
          while underneath the current curves left, or right.
Then Contentnea empties into Neuse, like an expansion
          of vision. A house on a bluff observes with its windows.
A red clay bank where they tie and eat seems as raw as
          a memory of fever. They hunch in the grounded boat and
open sardines, too hot to speak. Later, the water widens
          and pilings from long-disused landings protrude
from August's low water. They make camp on a sandbar as
          evening comes. The father watches his son in the canoe,
anchored in the channel-middle, as light all but fails.
          An invisible line quickens the rod with meaning.
The son, excited, reels in a flashing, hauls into air
          a quiver-sided channel cat blue as horizons over
bends. As they cook this fish on the Coleman,
          lightning bugs fill the trees that ascend from each
bank: galaxies of live stars. Cicadas and bullfrogs
          voice the winding-down of August. The man is
aware that the awareness that now lights in his head
          is as brief against galaxies as these pulses of light
made by insects. Tasting the fish, he gnaws a tear-salt,
          knowing his son no better than he knew his father.
The mystery of this teenaged boy, beginning to be
          muscular, good with the paddle, is seasoned by love.
Looking at the lightning-bug stars and the close,
          real stars, he feels his mind stumble to its limit.
He feels how love remains, and hurt, salt in a cut,
          and remorse, at the memory of a life unable to extend

its spark except unconsciously, in a love-touch that
    swallowed thought and made a son. Memory of his
grandfather's bottled water hangs before him in a globe,
    like earth's whole atmosphere. Vision has circled
from water; he imagines the earth and a cell and a child
    in membranes of wetness. He drinks from the bottle
they filled at Seven Springs, to begin this journey.
    The two beside the river are no longer visible
to one another. Father and son, they share the small
    tent, sleep. In the morning they are puzzled by signs
of sweeping. Beavers, clipping the willows, have pulled
    down branches toward the water, erasing footsteps.
For a little while more they print this bar with
    their shoes, before curving with the river into time.

Light's Praise

Light which is my being in the world
        while others aren't, how you strike
the leaf, which frost has thinned like skin
        (translucent to your probing, veined),
my thought still tender with the wound of
        what is not and what is yet. Light,
in my years left in the sun, let me rise
        within excitement, knowing, like a body
from a dive, breaking surface continually
        toward your pinpointed velvet,
your early coming to dew and birdsong.
        Harp me, responsive to your praise, permit
my lips, through your returns, to speak an
        awareness—extending to farthest stars,
from tissue of leaf lit green within.
        Light, existent from the start, not to be
extinguished by my or anyone's exit, circle
        on yourself, oh self-subsistent seeing, await
new leaf to illuminate. Infuse my doubt,
        glow in the sphere of your nature.

IX

A Voice in the River Park

Late May, and already trees have
siphoned streams, expanding massive
crowns that now seem the grave
of light. What the day has to give

is this climb up Cox's Mountain,
a blue vapor distancing leaves toward
the powerline-measured horizon.
The trail directs me downward,

where landscape folds into a vale.
I stop here, thinking with a thicket.
The hillslope trickles its intent,
deepening silence as in a well.

I look for the abandoned cabin,
find it by a ford. Smoldering years
have charred its wood and burned its tin
with rust. Then the river appears

below and I follow its plausible
turnings, where wagons from a mill
once wore deep ruts, that even now fill
with water for wind to ripple.

A current slips by me and is gone,
yet the stream continues. We're heirs
of a past we sometimes stumble on
when we follow the paths of forebears.

But can their figures be recovered,
to be faced all together and known?
I glimpse presences from before, gathered
a moment as within the dark screen

of my grandparents' porch, air
green with evening—their rockers
like pendulums, though the stair
between rushes longer than rivers.

A creek by our present house washes
and dashes on stones, gathers in pools,
where spring brings the fish
upstream to grow, before it spills

back into the Eno a mile below.
We've raised our family there, my wife
and I watching the current slow
for childhood, acknowledging life.

But nothing suspends its movement
for long. As I sit and write
after hiking and feel summer
almost here, it is almost night

for those grown gray in the porch screen—
honeysuckle sweet in the teeth then
too as green air holds again
those seeming strangers, women and men

I'm descended from. The place
of their voices becomes a cabin's distance
blackened by age. Those kindred faces
blur into soil, thinning with absence.

I'm sitting where children picnic. A mother's
singing from beyond the trees praises
these descending days,
crooning forlornly of *always*.

Botanical Garden: The Coastal Plains

for Dr. Marianna Breslin

Fever bark, chokeberry, and goat's rue gather,
a persimmon tree and bridge frame muddy water.
Beyond, in a dense tangle, fetterbush twines
wax myrtle the way religion grapples with sin.
Dragonflies complete the pocosin.
Raised above a muck, I let the scene sink in.
I've returned to a miniature of the terrain
where I was born. Sun again boils my brain
and pine needles sharpen their tips of pain
under snow-mountain clouds, those greedy breasts,
as one bruise-blue underneath now rests
over the pond where a turtle swims—
its below-surface shadow like an omen.
But tags are wired to stems. Plaques on posts
stand to explain, exorcising the ghosts
gathered in yaupon and pine. My father
is missing. Yet this land that entombs
my time has phyla and species, no longer dumb.
The secret dooms, once labeled, take on form.
The absent moccasin, as I now see him,
changes the meaning of his venom.

Autumnal Equinox

The earth has rotated again on an axis inclined from perpendicular
to the plane of the ecliptic by twenty-three and a half degrees.
Maple leaves in the canopy lamp back an acknowledging yellow
to a source in recession. Oaks higher up give themselves airs
in the wind, their lobed leaves handlike, sowers of generations.
They plop their acorns on my drive, turning heroically bronze —
inadvertent feeders of squirrels, as the dogwoods are of birds,
with their scarlet berries. These signals relate to one another,
a simultaneous response to progression through the altered rays.
Likewise my mind shines back a recognition, seeing these
leaves as banners on the billion-masted ship of Earth
as it sails in its orbit, with the sun in its galaxy,
with the galaxy receding from others. And this mind grows,
like the leaves, slightly dizzy, but wakes to a higher intensity,
that cannot explain such magnificent, pointless purpose, though
glowing within this medium of fruition and perishing.
Mind feels itself turn the colors of wonder: scarlet-maroon
with beholding, yellow with transiency, green in remembrance —
and looking into changes to come, a bronze of enduring.
Already, flags of lost summer spin aimlessly as the wind
grows chilly. Mind wishes to inscribe its thoughts
in a medium like the gold-amber sunlight. The light relates
these thoughts, those of the squirrels, seeing plenty, those of
the leaves, which parachute and spin, and those of this mind,
with its memories, which also wobble. The bronze oak
stands with nobility, in a firmament too blue for regrets.
A maple seed propellers down and lands on the roof
of my house, a blessing. The story is a continuing,
within changes so tragic, we can hardly believe this other:
this tale of sun-angle and colors,
of us and Earth in the conscious universe.

Letter to My Wife, from Minnesota

Supposing I never knew you, through those nights
when I fought to possess you, as a mystery retreated
while I panted into the roots of your hair?
The image and its motion, suffused with your irises,
slipped free as I worshiped with my lips and tongue
like a traveler parching on sandstone. Your nature
escaped as I gasped into my ecstasy, blue mirror
without center such as called explorers westward.
Now I collect our excesses in memory, storing them
like grain in elevator cylinders. I have buried
penetrations in your body's seasons, hiding intent
like warheads in silos. Your secret uterus eluded me,
yet you sang at the piano, a Mississippi or Ohio River
that ruffled its surface, reflecting the bridges and boaters
but iced-tea-dark underneath, skein of molecular
adhesiveness lank and sinuous, curling far headlands.
I have consented to your scent and sensed my undoing
over and over, yet arose and climbed the ladder
of my will, until my needs lost their guises in sadness,
wandering beggarlike below the towers they created.
I have wandered in the lost civilization of my mistakes,
expecting the ceremonial priestess who would sacrifice me
to her effigy. My allegory fails me, this instrument
paving over your impulse and hesitation, your wisps
of breath and moments, succumbing, when you who
were also often puzzled by what you meant
suddenly understood, conceiving new loves, and children.
Your fault is your limit of perspective, your passionate
locality. Your involvement was our children's lives,
like your focus of love on our grandson. You would
die to save him, as you risked death and unhealth,
bringing our three into the world. You do not wish
power in these concrete cities. You have come far enough,
you believe, when on our screened porch among sifting leaves.
Our grandson commands your attention and your body,
rolling his little locomotive or model car across your
knees and flanks and belly. I watch this miniature man

innocently purposeful, forecasting the play of his ambition
as he drives across your body that extends like a continent.
He will grow to master the freeways, will search into
an elastic horizon with his headlights westward.
Maybe later he will feel some other unpraised love
which asks not for itself and lets itself be mastered,
so that time may come into being, so cities may rise
and be dismantled—a love unseized in extent as it haunts
in sleep and in the sweep of rivers. It existed not even
in your figure, was some dimension undefined by coordinates
between navel and breasts and lips and vagina.
In the gist of bird-flight I breathed from your hair,
I inhaled generations. You have called me to your spaces,
like a pioneer urged to the prairie. I left my
moments of passion as marble headstones in iron-fenced
family graveyards from the South to the Midwest.
Such love lasts as long as eyes, a vision becoming language.
I imagine you speak it now, as your skin turns,
this yellow afternoon, into a parchment of our history:
each eyelash and wrinkle a hieroglyphic writing
from a world within the world, the time-scroll
we follow without knowing, punched paper that plays
on our piano the predictable ballads. These songs stay
below your skin. I see them there like the underlying
currents in the bridged Mississippi, like the grain
in our polished instrument. Nights, we play these old songs.

A Tapestry in a Mirror in the Palazzo Pamphili

Our features fade, consumed by the mercuric flame
        glassed in a Venetian frame. Behind, archers in
silk thread shoot arrows toward a tethered dove—neither
                hunters nor *amoretti*,

yet with piercing bows. And I feel the pang, a sharp
        loss in the chest that you whom I love best
reflect with me on the tattered weave. I see us recede
                toward its frieze: the puffed

sleeves unlike our tourist-cuffs but arms all the same,
        angled toward an object beyond us. For both a dust
intervenes, our faces superposed so that mine and yours
                take on the woven smiles of theirs.

Two mirrors opposed, the tapestry and glass begin an
        infinite regression, opening the wall into a cave. Down
this perspective, an African Adam and Eve
                have gathered a lunch of seeds

to plant our gazes, whatever millennia before, parent figures
        to be sorry for; like the couple in the Sistine ceiling,
so innocent, so knowledge-hurt. In yesterday's room of yester-
                years, we stopped before Narcissus'

pool: Caravaggio's, the satin flexing of his clothes a glow
        arresting sight, only the face caught in complete light
yet its opposite, soulmate, nearly lost on the surface
                of darkness. And he who thus

contemplates, his own face moved, is the artist.
        There he discovers his craft, his awareness in making.
And so we in recognition love, our likenesses,
                together, framed in his mirror.

Sailing the Inlet

My son and I are sailing toward
an inlet quick with changing tide.
Part of a current rushing forward,
we feel the moment intensified.

Whitecaps break the arced horizon
we angle for in a chilling wind.
Shallows and the chop of tide's return
promise and warn of what we'll find:

that hazardous space where gulls glint,
and landscape-perspective vanishes—
receding on any white wave-point—
as the sound with its houses diminishes

behind us. We tilt through an opening
that ends constraint of channel-bar,
careful of buoys, impatiently following
this fiercer wind past the final marker.

I've bequeathed my son this solitary
need to test self's strength against
a slate sea-rim—a jagged gray
in late afternoon. We tack, intent

on navigating northward, committed now
to the surfside cottage we will reach
if the light lasts. Swells lift and slow
our pitching hulls, that parallel the beach.

Vibrating with the tautly drawn sail,
we heel, then skim away from land,
pointing into dark sea only, until
distance behind us erases the strand.

We imagine the threatening surf,
where swells may lift the windward

hull as we shudder and luff,
to topple us both overboard.

Behind, on shore, my son's
new wife is standing to restrain us
from a vast run toward the horizon's
boundary, caught in the rush

of a wind-trance intending us danger.
My fingers, gripping the halyard,
remember fatigue. Again a father,
I return the helm to his strong hand.

Far on the strand, she lifts
her scarf where our cottage looks tiny
in dunes—where the sand drifts
slowly, like swells of the sea.

We ride in easily with breaking waves,
talking as men who have tested
themselves and recovered their lives
from ocean and wind. Bathed and rested,

we dine on shrimp that I and my daughter
prepare. My wife looks with delight
on sons and a grandson, as laughter
echoes around us. Late that night

I dream more sailing, with a glove-
close space in water beside, a touch
that follows like love, or a moving grave.
I feel the desperate, illusory stretch

of this traveling in time: obscure
route leading from rivers inland
to sea-horizon now finally pure,
in wave points past the arc of strand.

A Distant Father

Father, I saw you from St. Peter's Square, a tiny ivory
      carving in a chair—your amplified voice a part of the noise of
buses and tourists. You centered the spectacle, like the musicians
          at a rock concert, shrunken

below their special effects. So the façade behind, and dome, echoed
      you as only human. Yet you organized our gazes, like the places
beside the fountains from which Bernini's columns align.
          Your discipline held the faithful

while we others in Rome, to seek sights or art, moved restlessly on,
      drawn by the magnet of your museum. There the years filled
our gazes, Pintoricchio's *La Madonna col Bambino* enough
          to melt our hearts, Melozzo da Forli's

Angelo musicante plucking notes from a lute in thought,
      bowing the viola of heaven. And you are heir of all this,
Father, this bliss of canvas and fresco—and the judgment of great
          Michelangelo on himself and the race—

this flesh that later, lesser men disgraced with funereal diapers.
      Your predecessors under St. Peter's in neat, marble
rows seem volumes on shelves, beef in cold storage.
          This collection parallels the hells

that others supposed, from their frozen eternities
      of sculpted robes. Only Alexander VII is
rising from the folded stone, a skeleton with time in
          his hand: brass hourglass

where no sands fall. Father, in your giant home looming
      against the years, I hear an uproar as feet
from all continents whisk the inlaid pavement. The design
          stands firm, while we look from high

within your dome, upon multitudes winking their flashbulbs,
        as if fireflies some summer evening, no more bother
to your collective slumber than gnats to a mountain.
                        Fountains in your garden trickle

perpetually, jade into their basins. Your Swiss Guards stand
        stolid and tall while your frame fails and the time comes
when you will need a sculptor to carve your own figure
                        into this rock of ages. What better

fate can man want than to speak through this megaphone
        of years: this echoing palace of art and faith,
like the mouth-gaping tragic mask I saw in your collection?
                        A Titan composed of those

who've died, you embody a doctrine that oozes like bloody oil
        from the strata of centuries. The walls of Urban's brick
we saw descending the Gianicolo showed Aurelian
                        stone like the outcrop of a harsh

geological epoch. So you rise into view, a leviathan,
        like those giant Jurassic skeletons the scientists unearth
to puzzle us. We can't comprehend crucifixions, especially ones
                        inverted, can hardly conceive

St. Peter's bones buried below your altar. Yet there they were.
        In memory I see you again in your canopied chair,
and carefully chip away the extraneous silt, the tourist flood
                        you see as souls to be saved.

My eye extracts you, artifact of a faith molded in the volcanic
        convulsion hardened here in triumphal arch and Colosseum:
alabaster figurine beyond the crowd, where bones of holy fathers
                        underlie these heedless footsteps.

Interstate Highway

for our daughter, Lisa

As on a crowded Interstate the drivers in boredom
        or irritation speed ahead or lag (taken with sudden
enthusiasms for seventy-five) surging ahead a little by
            weaving between lanes but still

staying pretty much even, so too the seeker in language
        ranges ahead and behind — exiting and rejoining
a rushing multitude so closely linked that,
            if seen from above, from the height

of the jet now descending, we present one
        stasis of lights: feeling our freedom though
when seen from above, in the deepening twilight,
           the pattern we bead is constant.

So we have traveled in time, lying down and waking
        together, moved by illusions, each cubicle with
tables and chairs, beds where our cries arose
           lost in the surging engines.

Yet the roomlight where we made our love
        still cubes us in amber. Out of the averaging
likeness, Pavlovian salivation at the bell
           of a nipple, our lives extract their

time-thread, our gospel-truth. While Holiday
        Inn and Exxon populate the stretch
between Washington and Richmond with lights,
           I rewrite our pasts in this present:

recalling your waking dear wife, to find
        a nipple rosier, we not yet thinking *a child*
though impossibly guessing her features
           the feathery, minutely combed lashes

the tiny perfect nails, though not yet
        the many later trees at Christmas. Now
I know only backwardly, inscribing these sign-
                ings that fade as the ink dries.

Remembering the graph-like beading of darkness,
        I recall the ways that time once gave us—
distracted by signs for meals and clothing,
                travelers, heavy with ourselves

defining the gift that bodies carry,
        lighting the one, inner room, womb for
our daughter. Seeing us all from above, I read
                this love our child embodies.

Grandfather Wordsworth

You remembered waiting for the horses that would
        bear you to the death of your father—the day
tempestuous dark and wild, your companions
                  a single sheep, a blasted hawthorn.

Reinventing this proleptic sorrow, you knew
        the hanged murderer, a woman with pitcher
on her head, garments vexed and tossed
                by a wind of visionary dreariness.

This intensity sanctified loss, lifting violet by
        a stone into poetry. On Grasmere peaks
you climbed near stars, fathered yourself from
                the living nothingness past hearth fires

and language. You hated Robespierre,
        learned guilt, knocked sense into the gilded diction
of your day with "Sir Patrick Spens" and Coleridge's Mariner.
              Your voice spoke familiarly to me

from a school anthology. The scenes your words
        had painted moved, I knew from inside it another
climate and time. You inspired my first few poems—
              you and the good doctor Williams.

Next year, walking to Grasmere felt lonely
        and free, sunshine thin in late summer. Stephen
Gill at the museum outlined your favorite walk,
             William, with Dorothy: away from

Dove Cottage, around the lake, over a small mountain,
        and back. When I looked down from that peak
on Grasmere Lake, I felt complete. Words in my inner
             hearing spoke. Ancestors moved,

their moods raged and ranged in rain and
        blown mist. Grandfather Wordsworth, your wind
hit with sleet mixed in, rattling my poncho
                with a blast out of Scotland.

Wandering wherever it blew me I faced into ice,
        seeking the highest place, a farther pasture—
clambering stone walls, forcing my steps through
                gorse that pierced my socks

toward the tarn with sheep like wooly boulders.
        Clouds gone, rainbow over, I covered a scrawny
hemlock with my sky-colored poncho and walked apart—
                the wind then drying it, flickering it

into blue flame. The name then streaming my breath,
        William, held your name and my wife's
against the Atlantic distance. This banner
                of desire carried me to Liberty's

for a William Morris fabric, then to Windsor where I
        purchased the antique scuttle, once too dear as
we'd admired it, together. Casting love into these things,
                I winged with the quick days home.

The scuttle shines today on our hearth, worth more or less
        as we remember or forget. Men were *immortal*
and omnipotent, Shelley whispers, if *Intellectual Beauty*
                haunted us in permanence.

Did he ask if my gifts could recompense
        my wife for loving her intensely in absence?
We met at the airport, William, our embrace
                like Eve's and Adam's, after.

JAMES APPLEWHITE

is a professor of English at Duke University.
He has written many books, among them *Quartet
for Three Voices: Poems* (LSU, 2002); *Daytime and
Starlight: Poems* (LSU, 1997); *A History of the River:
Poems* (LSU, 1993); *Lessons in Soaring: Poems* (LSU,
1989); *River Writing: An Eno Journal* (Princeton, 1988);
Ode to the Chinaberry Tree and Other Poems (LSU, 1986);
*Seas and Inland Journeys: Landscape and Consciousness
from Wordsworth to Roethke* (Georgia, 1985); *Foreseeing
the Journey: Poems* (LSU, 1983); *Following Gravity:
Poems* (Virginia, 1980); *Statues of the Grass: Poems*
(Georgia, 1975).

*Library of Congress
Cataloging-in-Publication Data*

Applewhite, James.
[Poems. Selections]
Selected poems / James Applewhite.
p. cm.
Includes bibliographical references.
ISBN 0-8223-3601-4 (cloth : alk. paper)
ISBN 0-8223-3639-1 (pbk. : alk. paper)
1. North Carolina—Poetry. I. Title.
PS3551.P67A6 2005
811'.54—dc22   2005005703